Wineries
OF THE CAPE

SUNBIRD PUBLISHERS

First published in 2013

Sunbird Publishers
The illustrated imprint of Jonathan Ball Publishers
(A division of Media24 Pty Ltd)
P O Box 6836
Roggebaai 8012
Cape Town, South Africa

www.sunbirdpublishers.co.za

Registration number: 1984/003543/07

Design and typesetting by MR Design
Cover design by MR Design
Editing and project management by Michelle Marlin
Proofreading by Kathleen Sutton

Reproduction by Resolution Colour, Cape Town
Printed and bound in Malaysia for Imago

ISBN 978-1-920289-70-6
Ebook ISBN 978-1-920289-79-9

Although *Wineries of the Cape* endeavours to be as current as
possible, the dynamic South African wine industry is constantly
changing and growing, thus new wines may have been released
and tourism offerings enhanced since publication. While
every last effort has been made to check that the information
in this book was correct at the time of going to press, the
publisher, authors and their agents cannot be held liable for any
inaccuracies that may appear, nor can they accept liability for
any consequences or loss arising from the use of this guide or
the information contained therein.

Wineries
OF THE CAPE

The essential companion to touring the winelands

Lindsaye McGregor & Erica Moodie

SUNBIRD PUBLISHERS

CONTENTS

WINE TOURISM IN THE CAPE WINELANDS

In the mid-nineties I became involved in the wine industry, serving wine and conducting cellar tours at Delheim Wines in Stellenbosch. This is where wine tourism started – Stellenbosch was the first organised wine route in South Africa (circa 1971), and Spatz Sperling, owner of Delheim, was one of its pioneers. At the time the Stellenbosch wine route had fewer than 10 members – now there are 152.

Today there are 18 different wine routes in the Cape (including a brandy route) stretching all the way from the West Coast, right around the Cape to the South Coast and into the interior as far as the Karoo. The diversity of the winelands caters for all tastes and meets the expectations of gourmands and adventure-seekers alike. Coupled with our beautiful scenery, game viewing and numerous leisure activities, this is what wine tourism is all about – the experience 'beyond the bottle'.

The Cape is able to offer an outstanding wine tourism experience. This is echoed by the thousands of visitors who explore our winelands each year, and confirmed by our inclusion in the Great Wine Capitals Global Network, which consists of 10 members from the top wine-producing regions of the world. Rubbing shoulders with the best and exchanging ideas with other members of this prestigious network offers the Cape winelands the opportunity to elevate its image with the international wine tourist.

It is interesting to note that tourism trends correlate with our key export markets – there is a direct relationship between wine tourism in South Africa and the international sales of our wines. But wine tourism is not limited to the Cape winelands alone – it extends along our coastlines and also forms part of the game-viewing experiences at our lodges, and further afield into the rest of Africa.

As recipients of several Great Wine Capitals Best of Wine Tourism Awards, the Cape winelands have shown that there is something for everyone to enjoy along our wine routes. Over the last few decades, we have positioned ourselves aggressively as a premier tourism destination, with the wine and vineyard experience adding substantially to the broad tourism offering. We have become known not only for our fine wines, but also for our responsible wine tourism, and of course for the distinctive architecture and magnificent landscapes of our winelands, our art and culture, our fine dining and world-class accommodation, as well as for embracing technology and social media in innovative ways.

We have also become leaders in responsible wine production and stand out for our industry's commitment to sustainable practices – exporting the most Fairtrade labels, and establishing the Wine Industry Ethical Trade Association (WIETA) and the WWF-SA Biodiversity & Wine Initiative, which aims to preserve large tracts of our unique floral heritage throughout our wine-growing regions.

This book provides examples of some of the best we have to offer in the Cape winelands, all within an hour's drive from the Mother City, Cape Town. Plan and navigate your wine journey with abandon to the senses, but enjoy responsibly too.

Andre Morgenthal, July 2013
International chair, Great Wine Capitals of the World wine tourism commission

INTRODUCTION

The Cape has a long history of hospitality – it started out as a garden, after all, when Jan van Riebeeck planted vegetables in 1652 to provide fresh produce for the ships of the Dutch East India Company, which traded between Europe and the East. He planted vines too and wine was made for the first time at the Cape in 1659. Over the centuries, many travellers from around the world have savoured the fairest Cape's fine wines and food. Today, wine tourism is one of South Africa's top attractions, and enthusiastic and knowledgeable staff at wineries across the length and breadth of the winelands ensure visitors an unforgettable experience.

Wineries of the Cape celebrates the enormous diversity that the winelands have to offer. Cape Town, with its landmark Table Mountain, is the gateway to the scenic winelands and all the wineries featured in this book are within a 90-kilometre radius of the CBD and an easy hour's drive. Each region that we visited features one or more main focal properties – those that you really should visit to get a sense of place – and a few smaller wineries, each with its own special charm. There is something to suit all tastes.

Probably the most difficult part of producing this book was choosing which wineries to feature and suggesting which wines to sample – this is such an individual and personal choice. Boutique wineries that handcraft their wines are a natural fit for some, while historic estates are what others seek. The wineries chosen represent a diverse and exceptional experience, from the cradle of winemaking, Constantia, and the hub of the winelands, Stellenbosch, to rural Bot River and Darling, from old favourites with a colourful past to newcomers who are breaking new ground.

This book highlights a selection of our particular favourites, some visited over the course of a few decades. There are family farms that haven't lost their personal touch, stately properties that are centuries old, and newer contemporary wineries. What they all have in common is that they push the right buttons, be it offering a warm family farm welcome or proudly bearing an old Cape pedigree and affording an opportunity to view South Africa's rich and fascinating vinous history.

And there's so much more on offer than the brilliant wines: historic architecture; impressive art collections; magnificent gardens; exceptional restaurants and delis; and a variety of outdoor activities such as hiking, mountain biking, picnicking and trout fishing.

It makes sense to plan ahead when deciding which wineries to visit and it's always a good idea to check their individual websites first to establish if there's a festival or event taking place, as you may prefer not to visit on a very busy day. Also remember to double check on hours and public holidays as these do vary from farm to farm and change with the seasons.

ESSENTIALS TO TAKE WITH YOU
To ensure an all-round enjoyable experience, remember to take the following along with you:
- Enough bottled water – you'll need hydration, especially if you are tasting wines en route.
- A sturdy pair of walking shoes and socks if you are planning to walk in the vineyards.
- In summer, take sunglasses, sunscreen and a wide-brimmed hat or peaked cap.
- In winter, dress in warm layers (most venues have fires or heating indoors) and take a waterproof jacket, raincoat or an umbrella in case of rain.
- The latest *Platter's South African Wines*, a reliable and informative guide to the various wine regions and producers, complete with wine ratings and tasting notes, is an excellent companion.

Constantia & Cape Point

REGION: Coastal | **WARD:** Constantia

On the southern outskirts of Cape Town, only 20 minutes' drive from the city centre, lies the historic Constantia valley. Referred to as the cradle of winemaking, it was the site of Simon van der Stel's Seventeenth-century wine farm and has a winemaking tradition that dates back to 1685.

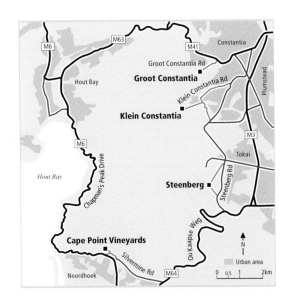

Over the centuries, much has been written about the legendary luscious sweet wines of Constantia, which were world-renowned during the Eighteenth century. They came to rival the great sweet wines of Europe and were revered by emperors and kings.

Along with the handful of historic wine estates in the Constantia valley, of which Buitenverwachting (established in 1796) and Constantia Uitsig (established in 1980 on a portion of Van der Stel's original farm) are also well worth a visit, you will find newer boutique wineries such as Constantia Glen and Eagle's Nest on this compact wine route.

The vineyards, which lie on the eastern slopes of the Constantiaberg, an extension of Table Mountain, benefit from the cooling sea breezes blowing in from nearby False Bay.

REGION: Coastal | **DISTRICT:** Cape Point

Accessed from Constantia via Ou Kaapse Weg, the acclaimed maritime vineyards of Cape Point, just over a kilometre from the sea, are situated on the western fringe of the narrow Cape Peninsula, at the foot of scenic Chapman's Peak and overlooking Long Beach at Noordhoek. This cool-climate district, which is often buffeted by strong winds and blanketed by mists rolling in from the ocean, is recognised for its Sauvignon Blanc and Semillon.

Also of interest
BUITENVERWACHTING **www.buitenverwachting.com**
CONSTANTIA GLEN **www.constantiaglen.com**
CONSTANTIA UITSIG **www.constantia-uitsig.com**
CONSTANTIA VALLEY WINE ROUTE **www.constantiavalley.com**
EAGLE'S NEST **www.eaglesnestwines.com**

CAPE POINT VINEYARDS

ADDRESS Silvermine Road, Noordhoek
(summer tasting room); No 1 Chapman's
Peak Drive, Noordhoek (winter tasting room)

GPS Summer tastings S 34° 5' 49.27"
E 18° 23' 4.94"; winter tastings
S 34° 5' 41.82" E 18° 23' 17.28"

TEL +27 (0)21 789 0900

WEBSITE www.capepointvineyards.co.za

TASTING & SALES
Summer: Daily 10h00–20h00
Winter: Mon–Fri 09h00–17h00; Sat
10h00–17h00; Sun 10h00–16h00
(closed on certain public holidays)

AESTHETIC One of the most beautiful
maritime winegrowing sites in the world;
relaxed setting for tented tastings and
picnics in summer

ATTRACTIONS Cheese/antipasti platters
(during tasting hours); picnics (only in
summer, Wed & Sat/Sun 12h00–20h00, Fri
12h00–14h00); Noordhoek Community
Market (Thurs evenings 16h30–20h30 in
summer, and Sun 11h00–18h00 in winter);
Fri burger nights (only in summer) – wine
available by the glass or bottle; nature trails
and vineyard walks; cellar tours (phoning in
advance is recommended)

MUST DO Make a round trip of it by
including Chapman's Peak Drive and a visit
to Cape Point on your itinerary

MUST TASTE Some of the finest examples
of Sauvignon Blanc in the Cape, made in
three different but equally focused styles

Cape Point Vineyards is situated on one of the most beautiful maritime winegrowing sites in the winelands. The vineyards are planted up the mountainside at the foot of Chapman's Peak in Noordhoek and from the vantage point of the tented summer tasting room, with its picnic area fronting a dam complete with a jetty, you can look out over the endless stretch of Long Beach and the Atlantic Ocean all the way to the Slangkop lighthouse in Kommetjie.

The first vines were planted on these steep slopes in 1996. The strong winds that blow in from the ocean, a mere 1,2 kilometres away, keep the vineyards cool, helping to keep diseases at bay and promoting a long, slow ripening period so that the grapes can be picked at optimal ripeness. As the vineyards comprise only 22 hectares with not much room to expand, viticulturist and cellarmaster Duncan Savage has focused on a select few varieties.

Although Duncan is a firm believer in traditional winemaking methods he also likes experimenting in the cellar, for example using 300- and 600-litre clay amphorae for fermentation.

Elegant wines with structure and intensity are the aim at Cape Point Vineyards, which focuses on three different styles of Sauvignon Blanc. There's the Cape Point Vineyards Sauvignon Blanc, the Sauvignon Blanc Reserve and a Bordeaux-style white blend, Isliedh (pronounced *ai-lay* and named in honour of owner Sybrand van der Spuy's first granddaughter). There's also a barrel-fermented Chardonnay in the Cape Point Vineyards range. The Splattered Toad range of wines, made for quaffing, comprises a Sauvignon Blanc and Shiraz-Cabernet Sauvignon.

In summer, more informal tastings with a view as well as picnics and functions are held in the tented tasting room in the vineyards. At the weekly community market with its stalls set up in the tasting tent, you can rub shoulders with the locals feasting at tables with one of the most awesome views and sunsets in Cape Town.

When the winter chill sets in, wine tastings move down the road to Chapman's Peak Drive, where the new cellar is situated. The tasting room is sumptuously furnished with comfortable seating, a tapestry from the 1800s depicting Bacchus covering the wall behind it, crystal chandeliers and an elaborate teak cabinet, which once belonged to Paul Kruger, who became president of the then Transvaal Republic in 1883.

GROOT CONSTANTIA ESTATE

ADDRESS Groot Constantia Road,
Constantia

GPS S 34° 01' 37,03" E 18° 25' 28,84"

TEL +27 (0)21 794 5128

WEBSITE www.grootconstantia.co.za

TASTING & SALES Daily 09h00 – 18h00
(closed on certain public holidays)

AESTHETIC Layered in a patina of history
and tradition, heritage preserved; Cape
Dutch architecture – oldest manor house in
the country, famous triangle gable

ATTRACTIONS Jonkershuis Constantia
Restaurant; Simon's at Groot Constantia
Restaurant; Iziko Museums of Cape
Town: Orientation Centre, Manor House
and Cloete Cellar; historical outdoor
bath; walks/hikes; cellar tours (daily
10h00 – 16h00, every hour on the hour)

MUST DO Stroll up the oak-lined avenues,
relax on a bench with views of False Bay
over the whitewashed *ringmuur*

MUST TASTE Grand Constance, a recreation
of the famous Constantia dessert wines
that were highly sought after in England
and Europe in the Eighteenth century

This estate, one of South Africa's most visited tourist attractions, is an important part of the cultural and historical heritage of the country. The entire estate, where winemaking has been practised for over three centuries, is a national heritage, fully operational farm. It is owned by the Groot Constantia Trust, which was formed in 1993 and is committed to preserving this national monument. Under its auspices, the historic bath, Jonkershuis complex and wine cellar were restored by architects Revel Fox & Partners. Also restored were the pediment gable and the graveyard, followed by renovation of the manor house, Hoop on Constantia.

Today, some of the finest surviving examples of Cape Dutch architecture in the country can be found at Groot Constantia. The pediment of the Cloete Cellar by German-born sculptor Anton Anreith is the most famous triangle gable in South Africa. Anreith arrived at the Cape of Good Hope as a soldier in the service of the Dutch East India Company in 1777 on the vessel *Woestduijn*. Anreith and architect Louis Michel Thibault are attributed with the building of the Cloete Cellar in 1791, which today houses a collection of drinking utensils and artefacts, as well as the remodelling of the manor house. Now a museum, it is furnished as the home of affluent people between the Eighteenth and early Nineteenth centuries at the Cape, such as former owners the Cloetes, and houses a superb collection of Cape furniture, paintings, porcelain and maritime art, portraying the early years of this venerable estate.

Groot Constantia is one of the oldest surviving trademarks in the world today, which is a testimony to its continuous winemaking tradition. The estate has won medals and awards since 1855 and still does so today. Groot Constantia is known for both its cool-climate whites and full-bodied reds.

Jonkershuis Constantia, a Cape-Malay influenced bistro-style eatery, is situated within the historic *werf* (open for breakfast, lunch and dinner Monday to Saturday; breakfast and lunch only Sunday). You can sit outside and enjoy wonderful views of False Bay and the Constantia valley, under vines in the courtyard, or inside where there's a double-sided fireplace for cosy eating on wintery days. It's also a popular teatime venue. Simon's at Groot Constantia (open daily for lunch and dinner) with its large, airy interior and vineyard views offers an extensive menu.

KLEIN CONSTANTIA ESTATE

ADDRESS Klein Constantia Road, Constantia

GPS S 34° 2' 19.0 E" 18° 24' 46.5"

TEL +27 (0)21 794 5188

WEBSITE www.kleinconstantia.com

TASTING & SALES Mon–Fri 09h00–17h00; Sat 10h00–17h00 (summer), 10h00–16h30 (winter); Sun 10h00–16h00 (summer only)

AESTHETIC A legendary estate, lovingly restored; custodian to some of the most historic vineyards in the world

ATTRACTIONS Collection of original Constantia wine bottles on display; estate honey for purchase; Vine Art Project – greeting cards, gift tags and Christmas wreaths; select luxury and limited release collectibles for sale

MUST DO Delve into the fascinating history of the luscious sweet wines of Constantia and the story behind the estate's modern revival of these famous wines; stock up on a few pots of their delicious honey, The Bees Knees

MUST TASTE Vin de Constance

The leafy, tree-lined driveway to Klein Constantia, situated high on the upper foothills of the Constantiaberg with views across the valley to False Bay, takes you away from the suburban bustle below and into the environs of a tranquil 146-hectare wine estate that was originally part of Constantia, a vast property established in 1685 by the first governor of the Cape, Simon van der Stel. He chose this particular valley for its favourable soils and mountain slopes gently cooled by ocean breezes from False Bay.

During the Eighteenth century the wines of the Constantia valley acquired an international reputation. They began to fetch high prices at well-attended auctions in cities such as Amsterdam and came to rival the sweet wines of Europe. "From these Elysian fields used to come one of the very greatest wines in the world – the legendary Constantia," wrote Hugh Johnson, "Constantia was bought by European courts in the Eighteenth and Nineteenth centuries in preference to Yquem, Tokay, Madeira ..."

Emperors and kings, from Frederick the Great to Louis XVI and the King of Prussia, vied for their share. Charles Dickens celebrated it in *Edwin Drood*, Jane Austen's character Mrs Jennings recommended it as a cure for a broken heart to heroine Marianne Dashwood in *Sense and Sensibility*, and Charles Baudelaire compared Constantia wine to his lover's lips in his most famous volume of poems, *Les Fleurs du Mal*. Napoleon had 30 bottles a month shipped over to St Helena to ease his exile.

In 1866, the dreaded disease phylloxera arrived at the Cape, devastating the vineyards and the golden age of Constantia came to an end. Its famous wines lived on only in the poetry and prose of the Nineteenth century and in the cellars of some of Europe's wine collectors.

In 1980, Duggie Jooste bought the neglected farm and decided to revive it to its former winemaking glory with the help of world-renowned authority on wine varieties, Professor Chris Orffer of Stellenbosch University. They went about studying early records and selecting vines that in all likelihood came from the original source grape variety, Muscat de Frontignan, and in 1982 the vines took root.

In the meantime, then winemaker Ross Gower and architect Gawie Fagan began work on the new cellar, which was finished just in time for the maiden vintage release in 1986. This was Klein Constantia's first new vintage for commercial sale in over a century. The wines were very well received, in particular Vin de Constance, a recreation of the original mythical Constantia sweet wine, which has since consistently appeared

"One of the Most Mythical Vineyards in the World ..."

French Institute des Paysages et Architectures Viticoles

on lists of the world's top wines. Even iconic leader and former president Nelson Mandela reputedly fell for its charms and ordered some cases for his presidential home.

More recently, the second book in the Shades of Grey trilogy by EL James, *Fifty Shades Darker*, makes mention of Vin de Constance, which has brought fans from around the world to taste and purchase the wine, and it is also alluded to in the latest James Bond book, *Carte Blanche* by Jeffrey Deaver.

In 1990 Duggie's son, Lowell, took over the reins of the estate and steered Klein Constantia through another two successful decades. During his custodianship the estate became a WWF-SA Biodiversity & Wine Initiative Champion.

Klein Constantia was bought by businessmen Zdenek Bakala and Charles Harman in May 2011, and in June 2012, respected Bordeaux wine luminaries, Bruno Prats and Hubert de Boüard, merged their Anwilka Vineyards in Stellenbosch with Klein Constantia, signalling the start of a new era of restoration and revitalisation, beginning with the manor house and to be followed by the cellar.

The estate's wines are tiered in three ranges – Marlbrook, comprising a classic Bordeaux-style red blend and an elegant white blend; Klein Constantia, encompassing the Vin de Constance, a Cabernet-led red blend, two Sauvignons, a Chardonnay, a Riesling and a Méthode Cap Classique; and the accessible, easy-drinking KC wines.

STEENBERG VINEYARDS

ADDRESS Steenberg Road, Constantia

GPS S 34° 4' 17.0" E 18° 25' 31.1"

TEL +27 (0)21 713 2211

WEBSITE www.steenberg-vineyards.co.za

TASTING & SALES Daily 10h00 – 18h00

AESTHETIC Bold, contemporary sophistication contrasts with meticulously restored Cape Dutch buildings, all set in manicured grounds

ATTRACTIONS Bistro Sixteen82; Catharina's at Steenberg; Steenberg Hotel & Spa; world-class golf course; walking trail; cellar tours 11h00 & 15h00 weekdays (no need to book)

MUST DO The 'wine and ride' – a two-hour guided cycle tour followed by a picnic and wine tasting

MUST TASTE Flagship tasting of the Ultra Premium wine flight, which includes a rare-in-the-Cape Nebbiolo, and their icon wine, Magna Carta, a seamless barrel-fermented blend of Sauvignon Blanc and Semillon

The first owner of Steenberg (Mountain of Stones) was Catharina Ustings, a feisty widow from Germany. She married Hans Ras, who was killed by a lion – legend has it that she hunted it on horseback and shot it; her next husband was killed by marauding tribesmen; and her fourth was trampled underfoot by elephant! After she took a fifth husband, Matthys Michelse, she got permission to lease the farm, which was formerly named Swaaneweide (The Feeding Place of Swans) in 1682. She took ownership in 1688, making her the first woman to own property in the Cape.

Catharina eventually sold the farm to a powerful and rich member of the Burger Council, Frederik Russouw, in 1695. He built the original U-shaped Cape Dutch manor house and also made the first wines at Swaaneweide. During the winter months, ships would dock in Simon's Town in False Bay because of the fierce storm winds in Table Bay. Steenberg was exactly a day's journey from Table Bay and equidistant from Simon's Town, which meant that many seafarers would stay overnight on the farm.

Over the generations the farm changed hands several times until it was purchased by Johannesburg Consolidated Investments in 1990. This consortium arranged for the painstaking restoration of the historic *werf* area of the farm. This includes the circa 1740 Manor House, Jonkershuis (young man's house), barn and the original wine cellar (now Catharina's restaurant, dedicated to the woman who pioneered it all). The farmstead has been declared a National Monument in terms of the War Graves and National Monument Act of 1969. A state-of-the-art winery replaced the old one in 1995, paving the road forward for Steenberg Vineyards. In 2005, Steenberg Hotel and Winery was acquired by the late Graham Beck.

Steenberg's marketing maxim 'Minutes from Cape Town, Miles from the World' sums up the ambience perfectly. Visitors can expect to be cocooned in style and comfort with slick service to match. The luxurious boutique hotel buildings, which date back to 1682, have been carefully restored and declared a national monument. Steenberg is one of only three working wineries with a golf course in the world (see Kleine Zalze on page 128) and the championship 18-hole golf course, which was designed by Peter Matkovich, fully utilises the natural features of the estate surrounding the hotel.

Visitors are spoilt for choice when it comes to wine tasting experiences, with a wine tasting bar, a tasting lounge with a cosy fireplace for winter, and an umbrella-shaded outdoor terrace with spill-over pools offset by a glass bridge and reflective water features, indigenous gardens with sculptures, and vineyard and mountains as a remarkable scenic backdrop.

Steenberg Vineyards was the first winery in South Africa to introduce its own application for all Smartphones, iPads and tablets, creating a convenient, internationally accessible interactive platform for the techno-savvy. The Steenberg range features a host of varietal red and white wines, blends and Méthode Cap Classiques, which are conveniently divided into categories, from Premium to Super Premium, Ultra Premium, Icon and Museum Wines. The Klein Steenberg range comprises a Cabernet and a Sauvignon Blanc. There are several different wine tasting options available, including various food and wine pairings.

Catharina's (open daily for breakfast, lunch and dinner), Steenberg's fine dining option, is named after the enigmatic first owner. The restaurant is housed in the original winery dating back to 1682 and offers contemporary South African cuisine. Seasonal menus feature garden-grown ingredients.

There's also the cellar-door restaurant, Bistro Sixteen82 (open daily for breakfast, lunch and tapas), an innovative bistro-style wine and food destination with a high-ceilinged open-flow plan. A unique Raw Bar with counter seating offers freshly prepared sashimi, gravadlax, ceviche, carpaccios, oysters and tartars. For a delicious experience, book a tapas and wine pairing in the boardroom. During the summer months (October to March), you can book a picnic basket – there are also boules sets and parasols available – and enjoy it on the lawns in front of the winery, under the Silvermine mountains.

Darling

An hour's drive up the West Coast brings you to Darling, where time slows down to an unhurried pace and warm country hospitality is a way of life. The village of Darling, with its restored Victorian homes on tree-lined streets, lies tucked away between vineyard-clad hills and wheat fields. Adjacent to the Swartland, Darling was once better known as a wheat-farming area until, in 2003, it was demarcated a wine district in recognition of the unique style and quality of wines grown here.

The vineyards, predominantly bush vines anchored in rich red soils, benefit from their proximity to the icy Atlantic Ocean some 10 kilometres from the Darling range of hills, which runs parallel to the coast. The area is known for the exceptional quality of its Sauvignon Blanc, and its highly sought-after grapes find their way into many of South Africa's award-winning wines.

The powerful Dutch East India Company, which set up a refreshment station at the Cape in the mid-Seventeenth century for ships sailing between Europe and the East, once kept vast herds of cattle and flocks of sheep on the grassy southern slopes of the Darling hills. These green hills still offer excellent grazing and Darling is known for the exceptional quality of its meat.

The village is home to many resident artists and performers, and there are art exhibitions, classical music concerts and year-round shows at Evita se Perron. Satirist, playwright, actor, activist and author Pieter-Dirk Uys converted the old Darling railway station into a cabaret venue where his alter ego Evita Bezuidenhout (also known as Tannie Evita, 'the most famous white woman in South Africa') performs regularly. *Perron* is the Afrikaans word for platform and also alludes to his inspiration, Argentina's legendary first lady, Eva Perón.

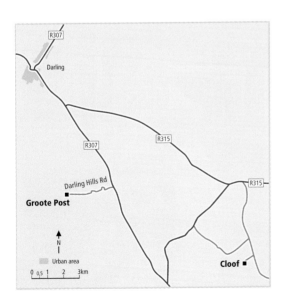

There are also flower festivals and the country's biggest eco-friendly music festival, Rocking the Daisies, as well as quirky coffee shops, well-appointed guesthouses, winery restaurants and several other tourist attractions, including the Darling Museum, which must surely be the best small-town museum in the country. Originally established in 1978 as a local butter-making museum, today it is housed in the old Town Hall on Pastorie Street and documents the history of the town from the 1800s, with fascinating displays from the Victorian era.

The area is famous for its colourful wild flowers in spring (from mid-August to the end of September

visitors flock to see this amazing display) and there are several wild flower reserves in and around the village. All of the wineries on the compact route belong to WWF-SA Biodiversity & Wine Initiative, assuring visitors of a relaxing and truly rural environment. Darling is also home to the critically endangered geometric tortoise.

Also of interest
BURGHERSPOST **www.burgherspost.co.za**
DARLING CELLARS **www.darlingcellars.co.za**
DARLING WINE AND ART EXPERIENCE **www.darlingtourism.co.za**
EVITA SE PERRON **www.evita.co.za**

SWARTLAND INDEPENDENT PRODUCERS

Charles Back's Spice Route Winery signalled the rediscovery of the Swartland in the late 1990s. Its winemaker Eben Sadie later struck out on his own to start the acclaimed Sadie Family Vineyards, leading a return to artisanal, natural winemaking in the area. He was joined by several winemakers and the resulting Swartland Independent Producers (SIP) is "the coming together of a group of like-minded producers working to express a true sense of place in the wines of the Swartland". The area is worth visiting for its ground-breaking wines. Almost all of the wineries are by appointment only, so it pays to plan ahead. The Wine Kollective in Riebeek-Kasteel is where you can stock up on the exciting wines from this region at cellar-door prices. The annual Swartland Revolution also takes place in the town in November.
www.swartlandindependent.co.za

CLOOF WINE ESTATE

ADDRESS Off the R315 (en route
to Darling)

GPS S 33° 28' 58.1" E 18° 31' 23.4"

TEL +27 (0)22 492 2839

WEBSITE www.cloof.co.za

TASTING & SALES Mon – Sat 10h00 – 16h00
(closed on certain public holidays)

AESTHETIC Rustic and relaxed with
wide-angle views across the vineyards
and wheat fields of the Swartland to the
mountain ranges beyond

ATTRACTIONS The Cloof Kitchen; cellar
tours (by appointment); wild flowers in
spring; annual Rocking the Daisies eco-
conscious outdoor music festival; walks
on Cloof and eco-and-game drives at
sister property, neighbouring Burgherspost
(booking essential); self-catering cottages
at Burgherspost

MUST DO Stock up on delicious Cloof
Kitchen preserves and chutneys to enjoy at
home with your wine spoils

MUST TASTE Shiraz and red blends

A dusty dirt road first leads you past Darling Cellars (worth a stop for tasting and picking up some well-made and well-priced wines) and then through bucolic paddocks dotted with grazing sheep for another five kilometres to Cloof and its sister property, neighbouring Burgherspost.

The vineyards on these Dassenberg slopes were first planted in 1966, with additional plantings a decade later and again in 1987. A cellar was completed in time for the 1998 harvest and the first Cloof wines were released during the following year. Plantings have increased significantly to 145 and 220 hectares under vines on each respective property.

The low-yield bush vines provide a canopy, shading the grapes from direct sunlight. A smaller crop – on average a mere four ton per hectare – results in smaller berries with thicker skins and concentrated flavours. The roots of the hardy bush vines go up to eight metres down in search of moisture, making them less sensitive to drought. Character building stuff – and the resultant wines with their quirky branding and funky packaging have tons of personality too. Make sure you take the time to read the cleverly written back labels on wines with names such as The Very Sexy Shiraz and The Very Vivacious Viognier.

The tasting room is rustic and relaxed, and there are plenty of versatile outdoor spaces from which to admire uninterrupted views across vineyards and wheat fields to the distant mountains. You can also enjoy a leisurely lunch (Tuesday to Saturday). A lot of the fresh produce used is organically grown in Cloof's gardens.

A philosophy of sustainable farming pervades both properties. In 2006, Cloof was named a WWF-SA Biodiversity & Wine Initiative Champion in recognition of the steps it's taken to conserve pristine natural vegetation and rehabilitate previously cultivated areas. Together, Cloof and Burgherspost have set aside 1 100 hectares for the preservation and conservation of the critically endangered renosterveld and sandy fynbos vegetation groups. While nearly 100 rare or endangered species have already been recorded on the reserve, yet more are being discovered as alien clearing exposes further fynbos.

Cloof's resident conservation officer conducts informative and educational game drives interspersed with photo opportunities that range from views of Table Mountain to close-up encounters with various buck and zebra. In spring you can book a guided drive to discover more about the ecology of the area and photograph the incredible floral diversity that Darling has to offer.

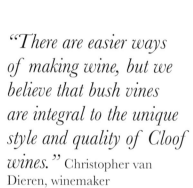

STACK 11A1
SHIRAZ
2012
14 X 225 = 3150

"There are easier ways of making wine, but we believe that bush vines are integral to the unique style and quality of Cloof wines." Christopher van Dieren, winemaker

GROOTE POST VINEYARDS

ADDRESS Darling Hills Road, Darling

GPS S 33° 26' 40" E 18° 24' 10"

TEL +27 (0)22 492 2825

WEBSITE www.grootepost.com

TASTING & SALES Mon – Fri 09h00 – 17h00; Sat/Sun & public holidays 10h00 – 16h00

AESTHETIC An oasis on the West Coast with a rich colonial history

ATTRACTIONS Hilda's Kitchen; game drives (booking essential); walks and hikes; bird hide; BYO picnics; cellar tours (see hours above); wild flowers in spring

MUST DO Go on a game drive or nature walk (book in advance); spot the prolific birdlife from the bird hide at the dam

MUST TASTE Consistent across ranges so follow personal preferences

At the end of a dirt road you will find an oasis with a picture-perfect *werf*, enclosed by white picket fences and complete with a historic frontier farmstead and a slave bell, which is depicted on the wine labels. The winery is housed in an old Dutch East India Company fort – Groote Post was once the largest guarding post in the area, set up in the early 1800s to protect cattle and sheep from marauding stock thieves.

The beautifully restored Groote Post homestead, which was built in 1808, was once Lord Charles Somerset's 'shooting box' and was later the home of well-known cook, hostess, amateur botanist and author Hildegonda Duckitt, who was born at Groote Post in 1840. *Hilda's Where is it of Recipes*, published in 1891, followed by her *Diary of a Cape Housekeeper* some years later, document early life in the Cape, including winemaking at Groote Post: "… the large vats would now be cleaned out, the cellars or buildings where the wine was made all swept and garnished, and got ready for the winemaking."

Dairy farmer Peter Pentz bought the farm in 1972 and later purchased two adjoining farms, including the equally historic Klawer valley. Today, the combined farms total 4 000 hectares. Some 30 years later, vines were once again planted on the property on the south-facing upper slopes of the Kapokberg in the Darling hills overlooking the cold Atlantic Ocean, which is a scant seven kilometres away. Their cellar was ready just in time for the 1999 harvest. In 2001, the Pentz family sold off their prize Holsten herd having decided to focus solely on the production of wine. Third- and fourth-generation dairymen, Peter and his son Nick have received many accolades for their wines since then. What's interesting to note is that these are consistent in quality across all three ranges produced here, from the top-tier Reserve to the Groote Post and the Old Man's Blends.

A member of the WWF-SA Biodiversity & Wine Initiative, over 2 175 hectares of natural vegetation have been conserved. In 1996, Peter Pentz was the first private individual to be awarded the State's premier conservation award for his major contribution to soil conservation over a 15-year period. He was also one of the driving forces behind the establishment of the Cape West Coast Biosphere Reserve.

There are plenty of outdoor activities on offer: nature walks in flower season, personally conducted by enterprising teenager Peter Pentz Jnr; farm drives through the vineyards and their 2 000-hectare game camp with its herds of indigenous antelope, black wildebeest, ostrich and quagga; and wildflower tours in spring. You can also take some time out to watch the prolific birdlife, including brightly plumed red bishops, from the bird hide at the dam.

The restaurant at Groote Post, fittingly named Hilda's Kitchen (open Wednesday to Sunday for lunch, booking advised) after Hildegonda Duckitt, the famous hostess who once bustled around the Groote Post kitchens, is housed in the Cape Dutch Klawer Valley manor house, which dates back to 1702. In summer, guests can eat alfresco on the *stoep* and front lawn.

Talented cordon bleu chef Debbie Mc Laughlin's modern country cooking utilises fresh produce, most of which is locally grown or sourced. The menu, which changes daily and regularly features favourites such as the Asian-inspired slow-roasted pork belly or homemade individual pies, is designed to complement the wines. There is an exception though – one dish that you'll always find on the menu is the popular Old Man's steak roll served with hand-cut chips and garlic crème. The 'Old Man' referred to is patriarch Peter Pentz and the dish was created to go with the Groote Post Old Man's Red.

Durbanville

REGION: Coastal | **DISTRICT:** Tygerberg | **WARD:** Durbanville

Bordering on Cape Town's northern suburbs and just 20 minutes' drive from the city, Durbanville is one of the cooler wine wards thanks to beneficial maritime influences. Cooling winds and mists off the Atlantic Ocean some 15 kilometres away and south-easterly breezes off False Bay in summer extend the ripening period, producing intense, fruit-driven wines. The vineyards are planted mainly on the rolling hill slopes in deep, well-drained soils.

Previously known as Pampoenkraal (*pampoen*

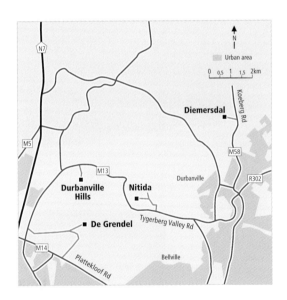

means pumpkin and a *kraal* is an enclosure) and named after a meeting place at a fresh-water spring for local farmers, it was established within a few years of the first settlement at the Cape. Durbanville once supplied the Dutch East India Company with fresh fruit, vegetables and meat. Although wheat and cattle farming predominated, vines were planted by the early 1700s. The valley was later named Durbanville, after Sir Benjamin D'Urban, governor of the Cape from 1834 to 1838.

There are several seasonal wine festivals in the family-friendly valley, including the Season of Sauvignon, the ward's signature white. Restaurants offer a range of eating-out options, from contemporary fine dining to relaxed country fare, and there are award-winning olives and olive oils available for tasting and purchase. Visitors can also make use of mountain biking and walking trails, offering views of the winelands.

The Durbanville producers are committed to conservation and initiatives are in place to protect the endangered renosterveld farmland.

Also of interest
DURBANVILLE WINE VALLEY **www.durbanvillewine.co.za**

DE GRENDEL WINES

"I don't aspire to quality. I am obsessed with quality."
Charles Hopkins, cellarmaster

ADDRESS Plattekloof Road (M14),
Durbanville

GPS S 33° 51′ 2.34″ E 18° 34′ 16.56″

TEL +27 (0)21 558 6280

WEBSITE www.degrendel.co.za

TASTING & SALES Mon—Fri 09h00—17h00;
Sat/Sun 10h00—16h00 (closed 25 Dec)

AESTHETIC Contemporary but with a long
Cape lineage; an 800-hectare working
farm on the city limits

ATTRACTIONS De Grendel Restaurant;
cellar tours (by appointment)

MUST DO Admire the iconic views of Table
Mountain and Lion's Head, Table Bay and
the Cape Town Stadium

MUST TASTE Koetshuis Sauvignon Blanc,
the signature variety of the valley; Pinot
Gris, a standout example from around only
20 varietal versions produced in the Cape

The first winery on the route and Durbanville's closest to Cape Town's CBD, De Grendel is set on the hillside and boasts one of the best views over paddocks and vineyards across the bay to the Mother City and its landmark Table Mountain, a drawcard for tourists and locals alike. The open-plan tasting room flows out onto the veranda to take maximum advantage of the ever-changing 270-degree panorama, which is spectacular at sunset.

De Grendel means 'the latch' in Dutch and was historically the gateway that had to be opened to cross the Tygerberg hills en route to the inland settlements of Durbanville and Stellenbosch. The farm was established in 1720, and the Graaff family have owned it since the mid-1890s, when it was bought by Sir David Graaff. It was used for the stabling of his Arab horses and later for the breeding of cattle and sheep. Today, the sight of grazing nguni cattle and indigenous goats greets visitors as they drive up to the winery, set high on the hillside.

It was his grandson, third-generation Sir David Graaff, a retired politician and one of South Africa's two remaining baronets (he inherited the title from his father, the late Sir De Villiers Graaff, who was the former leader of the United Party), who had the insight to plant vineyards just seven kilometres from the Atlantic in 1999, setting De Grendel on the path to becoming an established key player in the wine industry in a remarkably short time.

A carbon negative farm, De Grendel is part of a larger fynbos conservation area preserving the endemic but highly endangered renosterveld. A terraced indigenous garden utilises water-wise techniques. The cellar was designed taking the principles of Feng Shui into consideration and combines history with the latest technology. Glass windows allow visitors to watch the winemakers at work.

The blue-themed restaurant (open for lunch and dinner Tuesday to Saturday, lunch only on Sunday) also combines the old with the new. Porcelain under-plates are embossed in Delft blue with the family's crest. You can watch the chefs prepare farm produce, from freshly baked bread and hand-churned butter to free-range chicken and pasture-raised meat, in the modern glassed-in kitchen.

DIEMERSDAL ESTATE

ADDRESS Koeberg Road (M58), Durbanville

GPS S 33° 48′ 04.35″ E 18° 38′ 24.69″

TEL +27 (0)21 976 3361

WEBSITE www.diemersdal.co.za

TASTING & SALES Mon–Fri 09h00–17h00; Sat 09h00–15h00; Sun 10h00–15h00

AESTHETIC Gabled buildings set among quiver trees and tall palms; rolling hills covered in vineyards and wheat fields

ATTRACTIONS Diemersdal Farm Eatery, housed in the old stables; cellar tours (by appointment)

MUST DO Take a stroll around the beautiful *werf*

MUST TASTE The signature Sauvignon Blanc – several labels are offered for tasting, including the Eight Rows Sauvignon Blanc (when available), literally sourced from just eight rows of vines

This family farm is on the northern side of Durbanville on a scenic back road less travelled than the more concentrated Tygerberg Valley Road section of the wine route. Wine runs in the Louws' blood – six generations of the family have made wine at the estate since it was bought in 1885. The current incumbent is Thys Louw, who took over the reins from his father Tienie.

In 1698, Simon van der Stel granted this land to free burgher Hendrik Sneewind. The farm changed hands to Captain Diemer when he married the widow Sneewind and Diemersdal was established. An inventory, found in an old leather-bound book that dates back to 1705, lists 45 wine barrels, a wine press and glass bottles, indicating that wine has been made on the estate for over three centuries.

The farm covers 340 hectares with 180 of those under vines, which grow in deep red Hutton soils on the northern and southern slopes of the Dorstberg. The vineyards are cooled by mists that roll in each afternoon from the nearby Atlantic Ocean. The grapes are grown under dryland conditions (no irrigation is used), which allows them to ripen evenly and develop concentrated flavours. The rest of the farm is grazing land and renosterveld. This is one of the most threatened vegetation types in the Cape winelands and at Diemersdal they are working hard at conserving this valuable asset for future generations.

You can taste Diemersdal's range of classic wines in the cosy confines of the tasting room or at an outside table. Sir Lambert Sauvignon Blanc, their joint-venture with Sir Lambert Wines in Lamberts Bay on the West Coast, is also available for tasting and purchase.

The old stable has been restored and is now an atmospheric restaurant (open for lunch daily), where gifted chef Nic van Wyk (previously at La Colombe in Constantia, and Terroir and Kleine Zalze Lodge in Stellenbosch) serves up food offering the flavours of the countryside; herbs are from the kitchen garden, the pickles and preserves are homemade and the bread is freshly baked on the premises. The *plat du jour* lunch menu changes daily but Friday lunch is always classic bistro fare – sirloin steak with homemade chips. Saturday's menu features burgers, gourmet sandwiches and a salad of the day. You can also enjoy sunset tapas on a Friday evening (booking advisable) or a traditional roast with all the trimmings for Sunday lunch (reservations only). Diemersdal wines are available in the restaurant at cellar-door prices.

*"The homestead
itself is well preserved
and the palm trees
planted decades ago by
Grandfather Matthys
Louw whisper tales of
a bygone era."*

Thys Louw, winemaker

DURBANVILLE HILLS

"Everything is in our favour – the great soil, enough rain, hills and slopes facing the right way making them suitable to a variety of cultivars, and a wonderfully cool climate that allows the grapes to ripen slowly thus capturing a range of flavours." Martin Moore, cellarmaster

ADDRESS Tygerberg Valley Road (M13), Durbanville

GPS S 33° 49' 29.9" E 18° 33' 56.7"

TEL +27 (0)21 558 1300

WEBSITE www.durbanvillehills.co.za

TASTING & SALES Mon – Fri 09h00 – 16h30; Sat 10h00 – 15h00; Sun 11h00 – 15h00 (closed Good Friday, 25 Dec & 1 Jan)

AESTHETIC Clean ship-shaped lines with glassed-in decks for breathtaking views of Table Bay, Robben Island and Cape Town with its backdrop of Table Mountain

ATTRACTIONS The Eatery; Tasting Room menu (Tues – Sun); cellar tours (Mon – Fri 11h00 & 15h00; groups of 10 or more to book ahead)

MUST DO Try the wine and chocolate tasting but be warned, it's so popular that it often sells out, especially on weekends, or the wine and biltong pairing (booking advised for groups of six or more)

MUST TASTE Sauvignon Blancs, including the Rhinofields Noble Late Harvest

Durbanville Hills' slogan is 'Wines shaped by the landscape', a reference to the distinctive contoured hills surrounding this contemporary winery which, on a clear day, has remarkable views across the bay to landmark Table Mountain.

The venture owes its success to the enthusiasm and expertise of seven long-time suppliers to leading liquor company Distell, who launched the first wines, from the 1999 vintage, under the Durbanville Hills label in 2001. The member farms from whom Durbanville Hills winery draws its grapes are Bloemendal, Hillcrest, Hooggelegen, Klein Roosboom (the source of the fresh-water spring that prompted the first farmers to settle in the valley), Maastricht, Morgenster and Ongegund. Two more Durbanville producers from the farms De Grendel and Welbeloond recently joined the cellar too. The oldest member-grower farm dates back to 1688 and the 'newest' to 1714!

The cellar, which was designed and built to incorporate the latest technology into the winemaking process, houses 247 stainless steel tanks of varying capacity and can handle up to 8 000 tons, while still allowing for separate vinification of batches of grapes from different vineyards in smaller fermentation tanks. The tasting room has a comfy lounge area and opens onto the new renosterveld garden. The substantial wine offering is tiered in three ranges: Durbanville Hills, Rhinofields and Limited Terroir Selection.

Durbanville Hills, an accredited member of the WWF-SA Biodiversity & Wine Initiative and one of the first wineries in South Africa to recover, purify and re-use waste water, recently partnered with Wine to Water, a non-profit organisation based in North Carolina in the United States, which focuses on providing clean water to people all over the world.

The Eatery at Durbanville Hills (open for breakfast and lunch Tuesday to Sunday, and selected evenings), which was recently awarded a blazon by the influential international food and wine lovers' society, Chaîne des

Rôtisseurs, offers a modern bistro-style setting with an emphasis on fresh, wholesome local produce. Charcuterie and cheese platters are available in the tasting room. In summer (from October to April), you can head out to The Picnic Spot to enjoy an alfresco meal in the olive grove. Artisanal produce is served in hand-woven baskets, and bespoke blankets and comfy pillows are provided.

Durbanville Hills Extra Virgin Olive Oil, a peppery blend of Mission, Leccino and Frantoio olives, is made in partnership with nearby award-winning olive oil producer Hillcrest. Available for purchase at the cellar door, proceeds go directly to the Durbanville Hills Workers' Trust, established in 2000 to improve the quality of life of the workers and their families on surrounding farms.

NITIDA CELLARS

ADDRESS Tygerberg Valley Road (M13), Durbanville

GPS S 33° 50′ 38″ E 18° 35′ 37″

TEL +27 (0)21 976 1467

WEBSITE www.nitida.co.za

TASTING & SALES Mon—Fri 09h30—17h00; Sat 09h00—15h00; Sun 11h00—15h00

AESTHETIC Family-friendly and relaxed with panoramic views across Durbanville's vineyards to the Stellenbosch mountains

ATTRACTIONS Award-winning Cassia Restaurant; Tables at Nitida for more casual breakfasts and lunches; mountain biking trails

MUST DO Soak up the panoramic views over Durbanville's vineyards to the Hottentots Holland mountains in the distance

MUST TASTE Semillon in three guises – the single varietal wine, the blend Coronata Integration, and the Modjadji Noble Late Harvest

Nitida, with only 16 hectares of vineyards, may be the smallest farm in the Durbanville valley but it's also one of the most successful. Owner farmed and managed, the property is named after the *Protea nitida* (the *waboom* or wagon tree), which was historically used for making wagon axles, ink and traditional stomach ailment remedies.

Wine-loving couple Bernhard Veller, a chemical engineer, and his wife Peta, who was in advertising at the time, bought this piece of land in 1990, with the intention of making just a few barrels of wine. A few years later Bernhard took several weeks off work so that he could plant some vineyards. He was ably assisted by Klaas, who had worked on the farm for years and showed them the ropes when it came to milking cows and herding sheep, and powered by 'Pufford', a semi-derelict 1971 Ford tractor they found in the shed and learnt to drive.

Following a traditional and personal approach during the winemaking process, within three years they had made their first double-gold Sauvignon Blanc and a few year later they were recognised as a producer of benchmark Semillon.

There are two restaurants at Nitida. Stylish and airy, Cassia (open for breakfast, lunch and dinner daily) overlooks the farm dam and you can enjoy contemporary food either indoors or on the deck. Tables at Nitida (open for breakfast and lunch Tuesday to Sunday), a café-style eatery with an emphasis on healthy organic and free-range ingredients, also has indoor-outdoor seating options and is surrounded by lawns for children to play on.

Elgin &
Bot River

REGION: Cape South Coast | **DISTRICT:** Elgin

New cooler viticultural areas have opened up along the Cape South Coast region. The high-lying Elgin district, with its pretty patchwork of orchards and vineyards, lies cradled in a plateau in the ancient sandstone Hottentots Holland mountains approximately 70 kilometres south-east of Cape Town. Traditionally an apple-growing area, the region now produces wines showing exceptional complexity, elegance and

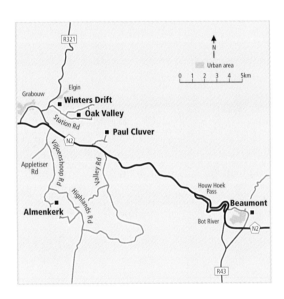

purity of fruit. Chardonnay, Riesling, Sauvignon Blanc, Pinot Noir and Shiraz do particularly well in this later-ripening zone, where the vineyards benefit from the high altitudes of 300 to 600 metres above sea level and cold temperatures with plentiful rainfall in winter, followed by cool south-easterly sea breezes in the summer months.

Several of the wineries are open by appointment only but are well worth a visit for the quality of their wines, including Catherine Marshall Wines and Shannon Vineyards. Others are closed on a Sunday, for example Iona Vineyards (tasting and sales: Monday to Friday 08h00 to 17h00; Saturday by appointment), which is a bit of a drive higher up onto the mountain slopes at the end of a dirt road, but worth the distance, both for the wine and the views back over the valley on the way. A series of Open Wine Weekends with various themed tastings and activities on offer once a month allows visitors to fully experience all that the wineries on the Elegantly Elgin Wine Route have to offer.

REGION: Cape South Coast | **DISTRICT:** Walker Bay
WARD: Bot River

Travel through the Elgin valley and you will come to the top of the Houw Hoek Pass from where you will get your first glimpse of a vast landscape of rolling wheat lands, vineyards and mountains, and the wide open skies of the Bot River ward, the gateway to Walker Bay and the Overberg.

The Bot River Winegrowers Association's credo 'Where real people make real wine' provides an apt description of the down-to-earth farmers on this rustic wine route, where you can enjoy real country hospitality and handcrafted

Also of interest

ELEGANTLY ELGIN **www.elginwine.co.za**
BOT RIVER WINE ROUTE **www.botriverwines.co.za**
CATHERINE MARSHALL WINES **www.cmwines.co.za**
IONA VINEYARDS **www.iona.co.za**
SHANNON VINEYARDS **www.shannonwines.com**
LUDDITE **www.luddite.co.za**

wines. The area is renowned for its cool maritime microclimate, which is influenced by its proximity to the nearby lagoon and Walker Bay. The wineries are centred within a 10-kilometre radius around the village of Bot River, with its winding Van der Stel Pass leading into the Bot River valley. Reputed white varieties for this area are Chenin Blanc and Sauvignon Blanc, and reds are Pinotage and Shiraz. Lovers of the latter should pay a visit to the artisanal winery, Luddite (Monday to Friday 09h00 to 16h00; Saturday and Sunday by appointment).

Both Elgin and Bot River are part of the Green Mountain Eco Route, the world's first biodiversity wine route.

GREEN MOUNTAIN ECO ROUTE

The world's first biodiversity and wine route encompasses family-owned wineries, country restaurants, delis and farm stalls, and accommodation. Part of the Kogelberg Biosphere, a World Heritage site, it is situated in the heart of the Cape Floral Kingdom, the richest yet smallest in the world and a biodiversity hotspot. All members also belong to the Groenlandberg Conservancy and are committed to conservation, sustainability and social upliftment. There's a four-day slackpacking trail as well as shorter leisurely walks, or you can explore by mountain bike or on horseback. Guided 4x4 or quad bike fynbos and birding tours, as well as abseiling and rock climbing in beautiful gorges are other options.
www.greenmountain.co.za

ALMENKERK WINE ESTATE

ADDRESS Viljoenshoop Road, Elgin

GPS S 34° 12′ 44.4″ E 19° 01′ 53″

TEL +27 (0)21 848 9844

WEBSITE www.almenkerk.co.za

TASTING & SALES Wed–Sun 10h00–16h00; winter months closed Sun (open on public holidays that fall within these days)

AESTHETIC Contemporary and inviting with an enviable cellar set-up and stunning valley views of mountains, orchards and vineyards

ATTRACTIONS Meals and picnics (pre-booking required, minimum 20 people) or BYO picnic; boules court; cellar tours

MUST DO Slide down the fireman's pole, the quick route from the cellarmaster's first-floor office to the cellar – but first get Natalie to demonstrate with the ease of a pro how it's done!

MUST TASTE The Estate range Chardonnay and Sauvignon Blanc; the Syrah for red wine lovers

Turn into the gates of this relative newcomer to Elgin and the wonderful views over the valley to the Kogelberg mountains beyond will delight you, as will the very friendly personal welcome at the cellar door, most likely from Joris or Natalie van Almenkerk. Everything about this venture with its showpiece winery speaks of careful planning and meticulous attention to detail, from the vineyards to the tasting room.

The Belgian-Dutch Van Almenkerk family's wine story began when Joris and Natalie moved to South Africa in 2002 and started the search for a farm in a cool-climate area where they could live and raise their family. After much searching they ventured to the Elgin valley and found themselves the proud owners of an apple farm in 2004.

Siting of the 15-hectare vineyards and designing of the cellar, which was constructed against the mountainside to take full advantage of the views, were implemented with the help of consultants and professors with a combined experience of over 100 years. They also used infrared and satellite imagery, soil samples and electromagnetic scans of the soil to ensure that the best possible site was identified for each different variety. In the cellar, a tank for each different variety and clone facilitates separate vinification. The first wines were bottled in 2009, and the growing portfolio includes the Estate range, comprising a Chardonnay, Sauvignon Blanc and Syrah, and the second-tier Lace range.

There are still six hectares of apples and pears left, and the landscaping of the mainly indigenous garden was done by fellow Belgian Dirk Vervaecke. They follow a nature-friendly approach to farming and use no harmful chemicals. There are 20 raptor perches on the farm and the number of bird species sighted has steadily increased, as has the fauna – there are Cape otters, caracal, grysbok, porcupines and a resident honey badger.

Joris makes the wines, Natalie is in charge of admin, marketing, sales and PR, and patriarch Joep, who recently opened a restaurant, The Brasserie on Beach Road in Strand, occasionally assists with wine tasting and sales, and acts as their business mentor. While the Van Almenkerks' approach to their business is seriously focused, they are self-confessed *bons vivants* and part of their mission statement is 'to have loads of fun while making wine!' Each year, a group of family and friends comes to help out during harvest and many meals, bottles of wine and laughter are shared together.

The Van Almenkerks conduct both a relaxed, informative wine tasting or a more technical one if you prefer, as well as cellar tours. A family member is always available to answer even the most in-depth questions. Vineyard tours and tastings for larger groups can also be arranged.

"*Guests are welcomed in our tasting room, which is really more like our living room!*"
Natalie van Almenkerk,
co-owner

BEAUMONT WINES

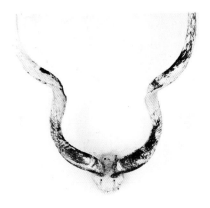

ADDRESS Compagnes Drift Farm, Bot River

GPS S 34° 13' 32.64" E 19° 12' 25.69"

TEL +27 (0)28 284 9194

WEBSITE www.beaumont.co.za

TASTING & SALES Mon–Fri 09h30–16h30; Sat 10h00–15h00 (closed on certain public holidays)

AESTHETIC Rustic and quirky, a family farm in the truest sense; home to the oldest cellar in the Overberg region

ATTRACTIONS Farm produce; a 200-year-old watermill, with limited quantities of stone-ground flour available for purchase; art and jewellery exhibits; walking and hiking trails; abundant birdlife; two historic self-catering guest cottages, the Eighteenth-century Mill House and Pepper Tree Cottage; cellar tours (see Tasting & sales for times)

MUST DO Book your place for the next Field to Loaf Day (contact the farm office)

MUST TASTE Hope Marguerite Chenin Blanc, a barrel-fermented benchmark

This quirky family farm is a bit off the beaten track but well worth a visit to experience authentic rural life in this small farming community centred round the village of Bot River. The Beaumonts' farm, Compagnes Drift, is steeped in history. Home to the Overberg region's oldest wine cellar, it was established in the mid-1700s as a Dutch East India Company staging post for those intrepid early travellers who braved the old wagon route, *Caepse Wagenweg*, and the crossing of the Bot River. It was a stopover and resting place where they refreshed their horses and oxen, and bartered for supplies with the Khoisan tribes and local farmers.

When Raoul and Jayne Beaumont bought the property in the 1970s it was a fruit farm. They once again planted vines and initially sold the grapes to the Villiersdorp Co-op. They decided to start making their own artisanal range of wines in 1994 in the old wine cellar with its antique basket presses and open fermenters. Initially Jayne made the wine, then Niels Verburg, who now has a farm and vineyards up the road where he makes wine under his own label, Luddite, took over in the cellar. Oldest son Sebastian, who graduated in oenology and viticulture from Elsenburg and returned to the farm in 1999, now tends the vineyards and handcrafts classically styled wines.

Founding members and part of the Green Mountain Conservancy, only 34 hectares of the 50-hectare farm are under vineyards; the rest consists of pristine fynbos-covered mountainside. The farm is on the Green Mountain

Eco Route – two mountain trails traverse it and there's abundant birdlife, including a pair of resident black eagles.

The farm is also home to one of the Overberg's most historic working watermills. It was painstakingly restored by Andy Selfe and now produces stone-ground flour, available for purchase in limited quantities at the cellar. Beaumont's 'Field to Loaf Day' is a wonderfully rewarding experience: the wheat is harvested with sickles and scythes, the grain is milled in the 200-year-old watermill and the bread baked in the wood-fired oven.

Sebastian's wife Nici and her business partner Jennifer Pearson operate Zest Catering (083 720 2202) out of the black-and-white tiled Zest Kitchen on the farm, with its vegetable and herb garden alongside providing fresh organic produce. Monthly lunches are held in the barrel cellar in winter (book via venue@beaumontwines.co.za) and the atmospheric venue is also available for private lunches, intimate dinners and celebrations (pre-booked, maximum 55 people; larger functions of up to 150 people are catered for in a marquee). Also on offer are cookery classes where you can learn some of the delectable tricks of their trade.

OAK VALLEY WINES

ADDRESS Off the R321 (direction
Villiersdorp), Elgin

GPS S 34° 9' 24.4" E 19° 2' 55.5"

TEL +27 (0)21 859 4110

WEBSITE www.oakvalley.co.za

TASTING & SALES Mon – Fri 09h00 – 17h00;
Sat & Sun 10h00 – 16h00

AESTHETIC A vast, established family farm
with a long-standing Elgin pedigree and
a growing reputation for wine excellence

ATTRACTIONS The Pool Room Restaurant
at Oak Valley; self-catering cottage;
mountain biking trail

MUST DO (If you're a cycling enthusiast)
The Oak Valley MTB trail consists of three
marked routes: a 14 km Green Route for
the family; a 24 km Red Route for stronger
riders; and the 32 km Black Route for even
more advanced riders. The trail has been
described as a five-star MTB experience

MUST TASTE Chardonnay, Pinot Noir and
The OV, a white blend

Oak Valley Estate is a large-scale mixed farming operation set on 1 786 hectares of prime land. There are 350 hectares of apples and pears; 16 hectares of greenhouse cut-flower production, making Oak Valley Flowers the largest supplier of fresh cut flowers in the Western Cape and supplier of choice to Woolworths; naturally reared acorn-fed pigs, and free-range beef cattle grazing on 583 hectares of open pastures.

The wine division currently comprises 30 hectares of vineyard with plantings of white-wine varieties Chardonnay, Sauvignon Blanc and Semillon, and red-wine varieties Merlot, Cabernet Sauvignon, Cabernet Franc, Merlot, Pinot Noir and Shiraz.

Oak Valley Estate was founded in 1898 by Sir Antonie Viljoen, a medical doctor who graduated from Edinburgh University in Scotland. He was also a Senator in the Cape Parliament and was knighted in 1916 for his efforts to reconcile Boer and Brit after the South African War. Having signed up as a medical officer with the Boer army during the war, Sir Antonie was placed under house arrest on Oak Valley for the remainder of the campaign after his capture by the British. His internment was granted only on condition that he paid for the services of two British soldiers to guard him for the duration of the war.

Up until that time, the Elgin valley was deemed to have little agricultural potential but Sir Antonie soon changed that perception. He was a highly successful farmer and among his many notable achievements was establishing the first commercial deciduous fruit orchards in the valley. This led to the development of the apple industry in Elgin, which to this day is the economic backbone of the valley. He also planted a substantial area of vineyard, followed in 1908 by the commissioning of the very first wine cellar in the Elgin valley. This was unfortunately taken out of production in the early 1940s. He loved trees and established large forests of English oaks. His will specified that no future inheritor of the property would be allowed to cut any of these down and today there are over 4 000 oak trees covering 30 hectares of the farm.

Oak Valley, a founder member of the Green Mountain Eco Route, was nominated as the ninth champion under the WWF-SA Biodiversity & Wine Initiative in recognition of the ongoing protection and conservation of its botanical heritage. Oak Valley was also the winner of the inaugural 2009 Nedbank Green Awards for Best Environmental Practices within the South African wine industry.

Anthony Rawbone-Viljoen has been farming the property since 1973 and it was during his tenure that winegrowing was reintroduced to the estate. His son Christopher, who graduated with a Masters in Wine Business from Adelaide University in Australia, recently introduced a restaurant-deli and wine tasting centre, known as The Pool Room.

The airy Pool Room (open for lunch Tuesday to Sunday, and for dinner on Friday and Saturday), with its deli and tasting counter, overlooks the pool and terrace, offering views of lovely tree-shaded gardens and a mountain backdrop. The restaurant offers a relaxed environment and delicious country-inspired food with a Mediterranean slant. Ingredients are sourced mainly from the farm: there's free-range grass-fed beef and acorn-fed pork; charcuterie, including Iberico-styled ham; seasonal vegetables and herbs from the garden behind the kitchen; and artisanal breads baked in the wood-burning oven. The farm's Wagyu beef (better known as Kobe beef in Japan) is also on offer at the restaurant from time to time, depending on availability. Estate wines are complemented by Cap Classique and Champagne.

PAUL CLUVER ESTATE WINES

The down-to-earth Clüvers own this family-run winery in the cool-climate Elgin ward. The close-knit clan's roots at their estate, De Rust, go back to 1896 and they remain central to its continuing success. They first started making wine on the estate in 1997.

Four of the five siblings are involved in the business, taking over the reins from their parents, neurosurgeon Dr Paul Clüver and his wife Songvei. Paul Jnr is managing director, Liesl is marketing director, Inge is financial manager (and married to Andries Burger, the winemaker) and Karin is the production director of the orchards. Craig Harris is the vineyard manager and his wife, Jacqueline, is part of the marketing team. There are 75 hectares of vines and the focus is on Chardonnay, Pinot Noir and Riesling.

There are also apple and pear orchards, a Hereford stud and various eco-tourism activities, including the amphitheatre with its Summer Festival Programme of concerts under the stars. Tall eucalyptus trees encircle the open-air timber-hewn arena, creating an intimate setting that seats only 600 people and makes it possible for guests to interact with the performing artists.

The amphitheatre is situated in the Cluver Family Reserve, which is part of the UNESCO-registered Kogelberg Biosphere Reserve, a World Heritage site. The reserve, where bontebok, impala, springbok, zebra and ostriches breed, takes up 400 hectares. In total, 1 200 hectares have been set aside for conservation. The Cluvers also launched The Doctor's Corridor, an innovative initiative to establish an ecological passage on the estate.

A visionary with a pioneering spirit, Dr Clüver was instrumental in developing the Groenlandberg Conservancy, which spans 34 000 hectares, and the estate is a founder member of the Green Mountain Eco Route. He is also a founding signatory of WWF-SA Biodiversity & Wine Initiative and the Clüvers' estate achieved BWI Champion status in 2009. In 2010, the Lifetime Achievement Award in the Drinks Business Green Awards went to Dr Clüver, and Paul Cluver Estate Wines was a joint runner-up in the Ethical Company Award.

The country restaurant on the estate, Fresh, is open Tuesday to Saturday for lunch (closed in winter from June to August). The menu changes seasonally according to what is available in the nearby herb and vegetable garden, which was started some years ago by Dr Clüver and Norwegian celebrity chef Andreas Viestad.

De Rust Estate is also home to the Elgin Distilling Company. The distillery houses a gleaming copper Cognac-style potstill where Malus, a hand-crafted limited-release spirit made from apples, is produced.

WINTERS DRIFT

ADDRESS Off the R321, Elgin

GPS S 34° 08' 59.42" E 19° 02' 22.61"

TEL +27 (0)21 859 3354

WEBSITE www.wintersdrift.com

TASTING & SALES Tues – Fri 09h00 – 16h00;
Sat 10h00 – 16h00; open first Sun
every month (other Sun and Mon by
appointment)

AESTHETIC Old-world charm, nostalgic
with an air of the romance of bygone days

ATTRACTIONS Tasting is in the restored
Elgin train station; Platform 1 Eatery (light
lunches and picnics available)

MUST DO Visit in winter when the
mountains are capped with snow and
there's a fire to warm yourself at in the
cosy Waiting Room; in summer, relax on a
bench on the tree-shaded platform

MUST TASTE The Chardonnay and
Sauvignon Blanc are proving popular

Worth a stopover on the way to Oak Valley Estate (see page 52) is Winters Drift's Tasting Station in the Elgin station building on Glen Elgin wine farm, where the wines are grown. Winters Drift is the wine brand of farming operation Molteno Brothers (Pty) Ltd. The first vines, which now total 54 hectares, were planted in 2004, and the first own-label wines were made in 2010 at the Gabriëlskloof cellar in Bot River, with the nearby Spioenkop Wines being added for later vintages.

Molteno Brothers leased the station buildings and restored them. The old railway line runs through the farm and goods trains still trundle past twice a day. In the tasting room, complete with its counter made from Jarrah wood, stationmasters' peaked caps hang from brass hooks and seating is on wooden benches or at café tables. The other room with its 'Waiting Room' sign has a comfy couch and armchair in front of the original brick fireplace. A framed map on the wall indicates the farm's original boundaries, as well as the ford used in winter to cross the Palmiet River from which the wine brand takes its name. This ford was part of the original ox wagon trail through the Overberg.

The wines offer easy drinking at pleasing prices, and chewy dried apple rings in branded brown paper bags accompany them. Dried fruits, as well as fresh produce from Glen Elgin and other local producers, delicious honey, cut fynbos and potted proteas, are all available for purchase in the deli at the Tasting Station. Light lunches and picnics are also on offer.

Pioneering bachelor brothers Ted and Harry Molteno have left a remarkable legacy. Sons of John Molteno, the first premier of the Cape, they purchased Glen Elgin in 1903 and transformed it from a modest vegetable farm into a vast fruit-farming enterprise. In the tasting room today, the old station clock keeps accurate time, while the antique mantle clock, which kept time in the brothers' house for over 80 years, has been stopped at 19h03, commemorating the year that they bought Glen Elgin.

Ted passed away in 1950 and his brother Harry followed him to the grave in 1969. His will confirmed their earlier decision that the profits from Glen Elgin would be channelled into South African charitable, cultural and educational projects. These include endowments at Cape universities and what was known as the Molteno Project for the advancement of the English language among scholars who speak a different home language (today known as Molteno Institute for Language and Literacy), as well as school bursary schemes.

Winters Drift is a proud WWF-SA Biodiversity & Wine Initiative Champion, as well as a member of the Groenlandberg Conservancy and the Green Mountain Eco Route.

ELGIN
MYL NA
KAAPSTAD
51 MILES TO
CAPE TOWN

*"The wines from
the region are low
in sugar and have a
higher acidity. This is
important as it means
the wines keep longer."*
Emy Matthews, marketing and
Tasting Station manager

Franschhoek

REGION: Coastal | **DISTRICT:** Franschhoek Valley

The beautiful Franschhoek valley has a marked French ambience and tradition all its own. It was settled by French Huguenots in 1688, who brought with them their food and wine culture. They were given land to farm in this valley, enclosed on three sides by towering mountains and known as Olifantshoek (Elephant's Corner) as vast herds roamed the area. Their annual migration wore a path over the mountain, which became known as Elephant's Pass and is today the scenic Franschhoek Pass. The enclave was first known as Le Quartier Français (the French Quarter), but was later named Franschhoek (French Corner).

The valley has retained its French Huguenot character. Some of the farms established then are still owned and worked by the descendants of the original owners, and as you drive into the valley you will notice that many of the farms still proudly bear their original French names. The Huguenot Memorial Monument at the top end of the village commemorates their heritage and the Huguenot Museum next to it chronicles their history. The charming village with its bustling main road is lined with restaurants and street cafés, boutique hotels and guesthouses, art galleries and specialist shops.

For an eagle-eye view over the valley, visit La Petite Ferme Winery on the Franschhoek Pass. In-depth tastings (by appointment only every day from 11h00) at this boutique winery and country restaurant are conducted by owner-winemaker Mark Dendy-Young or his father. After lunch you can enjoy afternoon tea or opt for a bottle of wine and relax on a bench or laze on the lawn to enjoy the stunning vistas. For a totally different perspective, you can take the road less travelled – a back road, Robertsvlei (much of which is a dirt road). It takes you through a secluded valley,

where you can start at GlenWood, which now boasts Okamai, a Japanese cuisine and sushi eatery, and end up at the boutique winery, La Bri Estate. Back in the village is Colmant Cap Classique & Champagne (by appointment only), a must for lovers of bubbly. Franschhoek is home to many other top sparkling wine producers and has its own Cap Classique Route (see opposite).

Franschhoek is, of course, also a great destination for flyfishing in the Berg River. Farmed in the valley, salmon trout is available fresh, hot and cold smoked, or cured.

Also of interest
ARTISAN FOOD ROUTE **www.franschhoek.org.za**
GLENWOOD **www.glenwoodvineyards.co.za**
LA BRI ESTATE **www.labri.co.za**
LA PETITE FERME WINERY **www.lapetiteferme.co.za**
VIGNERONS DE FRANSCHHOEK **www.franschhoek.org.za**

In the valley you will also find small-scale artisan producers, who are as focused and passionate as their winemaking counterparts, making everything from bread to cheese, olive oil, jams, pickles and preserves. The recently launched Franschhoek Artisan Food Route currently links 22 of these producers.

Many of the Franschhoek producers are members of WWF-SA Biodiversity & Wine Initiative and are committed to the conservation of the natural fynbos, some species of which are indigenous only to the valley.

FRANSCHHOEK CAP CLASSIQUE ROUTE

Good news for lovers of bubbly was the re-launch of the Franschhoek Cap Classique Route in 2012. The first of its kind in the country, this niche route links 18 Méthode Cap Classique producers in the Franschhoek Valley, which is renowned for its outstanding sparkling wines made according to the traditional method in a diverse range of styles. The route extends from Simondium through the valley and village all the way up to the Franschhoek Pass. **www.franschhoek.org.za/routes/franschhoek_cap_classique_route/**

BOEKENHOUTSKLOOF WINERY

This boutique winery in the furthest corner of the Franschhoek valley is one of the oldest farms in the area. It was established in 1776 and its name means 'Ravine of the Boekenhouts', an indigenous Cape beechwood tree that was highly prized for furniture making – these trees still flourish on the farm today. The label on the Boekenhoutskloof range of wines features seven period chairs dating back to the Eighteenth century and pays tribute to the skills of those craftsmen. The chairs also represent the owners, a group of six advertising and business executives, and winemaker Marc Kent, the seventh director, who bought the property in 1993.

The first wines released were from the 1996 vintage and they immediately impressed critics. Boekenhoutskloof was the Platter's South African Wine Guide Winery of the Year 2012 "for their understated but highly influential role in placing South Africa on the international fine-wine map" and having collected the most five-star wines of all the Franschhoek wineries over the history of the Platter guide, a remarkable 14 five-star ratings stretching back to its 2000 edition. The legendary Boekenhoutskloof Syrah 1997, the maiden release, is undoubtedly one of the most important benchmarks of the modern winemaking era of South Africa.

The consistently exceptional Boekenhoutskloof range comprises the aforementioned Syrah, a Cabernet Sauvignon, Semillon, Semillon Noble Late Harvest and a Cabernet Franc-based Bordeaux-style blend. The Semillon is produced from Franschhoek bush vines, a block of which is over a century old. Only a few barrels of the Sauternes-style Semillon Noble Late Harvest are made; and even rarer is The Journeyman, a Bordeaux-style blend, which was made only in 2005, 2007, 2009 and 2011. The focus remains firmly on quality, despite an exponential increase in quantity.

The modern tasting room spills out onto a patio to take maximum advantage of the setting with its vineyards and towering mountains. The outside tasting area is dominated by a giant porcupine: called 'Protection', it's a sculptural work by land artist Simon Max Bannister, who was named the David Shepherd Wildlife Foundation's Wildlife Artist of the Year for 2013.

While only a few of the Boekenhoutskloof wines, which make up only one per cent of production, are occasionally available for tasting (but not for purchase; they are booked in advance and sold out on release), on offer in the tasting room are their three other much-loved brands, all of which consistently over-deliver: The Chocolate Block, Porcupine Ridge and The Wolftrap.

The Chocolate Block, a multi-regional Shiraz-led red blend, is a stand-alone wine (that is, not part of a range). The maiden vintage 2002 constituted a mere 15 barrels. Today, it literally flies out of the tasting room and is arguably South Africa's leading premium brand of the last decade.

Made to be drunk young, the Porcupine Ridge wines nonetheless resemble the flagship wines in style. Two-thirds of the range is the ever-popular Sauvignon Blanc, one of the best-selling Sauvignons in the country. There are three red varietal wines – Cabernet Sauvignon, Merlot and Syrah – and two Rhône-style blends: a Syrah-Viognier and a Viognier-Grenache Blanc.

The range is named after the crested porcupine, an inhabitant of the farm and the subject of a research project by a PhD student, who recorded their feeding behaviour and movement patterns. Invasive alien plants are being removed, and restoration of the riverine area and the reintroduction of various protea species remain ongoing. A rare Erica, *Erica lerouxiae*, which is endemic to Boekenhoutskloof and the neighbouring farm, has been identified on the property. Boekenhoutskloof is a founder member of the Franschhoek Mountain Conservancy, an initiative to improve co-operation between neighbours, as well as fire management and fynbos conservation in the valley.

The Wolftrap wines are all made from Rhône varieties and offer good-value enjoyment. They are named after an old wolf trap that was found on the farm, but apparently there have been no reported sightings of wolves on the farm in recent times. The Wolftrap Red is a Mourvèdre, Syrah and Viognier blend; the Wolftrap White is a blend of Chenin Blanc, Grenache Blanc and Viognier; and the Rosé is made from Syrah, Cinsault and Grenache.

BOSCHENDAL WINES

ADDRESS Pniel Road (R310), Groot
Drakenstein, Franschhoek

GPS S 33° 52' 27.5" E 18° 58' 34.4"

TEL +27 (0)21 870 4200

WEBSITE www.boschendalwines.com

TASTING & SALES Daily: May–Oct
09h00–16h30; Nov–Apr 10h00–16h00
(closed on certain public holidays)

AESTHETIC Gracious, with a heritage
stretching back to the French Huguenots;
added attention and recent renovations
under new ownership have restored lustre

ATTRACTIONS The Restaurant and Wine Bar;
Le Café; Le Pique Nique for sunny days or
starlit picnics on the lawns of the famous
Le Pavillon; the Manor House Museum; The
Waenhuiswinkel (The Coach House Store), a
gift and wine shop; internationally acclaimed
rose garden; herb garden; cellar tours (daily
at 10h30, 11h30 & 15h00)

MUST DO Visit the Manor House Museum
for a glimpse into a bygone era; pre-book
a drive up to the viewpoint (you will pass
Rhodes' cottage en route) for a tasting
with a difference

MUST TASTE Wine ranges cover all bases
from reds and whites to sparkling, so
be guided by your own personal taste
preferences

One of the oldest wine estates in South Africa, Boschendal offers the quintessential Cape winelands experience, drawing people from around the world and attracting an average of some 300 visitors a day during the height of season. Many come to see the Cape Dutch vernacular architecture, while others are drawn to the famous rose and herb gardens.

The title deed for 'Bossendaal' ('wood and dale' in Dutch) identifies the first owner as French Huguenot Jean le Long from as far back as 1685. The farm was acquired by the De Villiers family in 1715 and it was during their tenure that it became a prosperous wine farm. A new homestead was built by Jean de Villiers, out of necessity no doubt to house his 22 children, along with outhouses including quarters for the 31 slaves he owned. His son Paul rebuilt the manor house in its present form and the date 1812 appears on the gable along with his and his wife's initials.

Following the devastation caused by phylloxera in the vineyards, the mining magnate Cecil John Rhodes acquired a score of old Huguenot farms, including Boschendal, and established Rhodes Fruit Farms (RFF) in the valley. A cottage, designed for him by Herbert Baker, still stands today. Unfortunately Rhodes died in 1902 and it is unlikely that he ever stayed there. The De Beers mining company continued to manage RFF for another 40 years until they sold the farming operation to Sir Abe Bailey. In the 1950s and 60s a syndicate took ownership of RFF and ran it productively as a fruit farm.

An extensive redevelopment programme, with a focus on winemaking, was initiated by the Anglo American Corporation, which took over in 1969. In 1973, Boschendal's original farmstead was restored and renovated; it was declared a national monument and reopened to the public in 1976. A typically H-shaped manor house with its yellowwood ceilings, floorboards and doors set in teak frames, it is one of only a few original Cape farmsteads to have been restored and furnished according to old inventories. The finest available plant material revitalised the vineyards and a substantial investment in the cellars raised the quality of the wines.

A consortium took over from Anglo American in 2003 and, at the end of 2012, new owners, trading under the company name of Canombys, began restoring the historic property (which is being considered for UNESCO World Heritage status as a cultural landscape) to its former splendour.

Boschendal is a member of the WWF-SA Biodiversity & Wine Initiative. Almost half of the 2 240-hectare estate has been set aside for conservation and there's an environmental management strategy in place.

The 250-hectare vineyards extend an impressive six kilometres along

the Groot Drakenstein slopes, and are predominantly planted to red-wine varieties Cabernet Sauvignon, Merlot and Shiraz and to white-wine varieties Chardonnay and Sauvignon Blanc.

The cellar for Le Rhône, built in 1837, has been incorporated into the state-of-the-art winery which features a dedicated red-wine cellar and a separate white-wine cellar. The Boschendal wine brand is owned by DGB (Pty) Ltd. The wines are styled to be classic with a modern New World approach and encompass a Cap Classique range, as well as the Cecil John Reserve range, the Reserve Collection, and the 1685, Classic, Elgin and The Pavilion ranges. In 1981, Boschendal was the first winery in the Cape to produce a Blanc de Noir, a pink-hued wine made in a white-wine style from red-wine grapes. Today, Boschendal's Blanc de Noir remains the best seller in this category.

There's a new tasting bar adjacent to the museum and adjoining the restaurant but the tasting facility itself is housed in the oldest building on the farm, which may have served as a coach house or as stables at some stage. Called the Cellar Door, it is a two-minute drive through vineyards and fruit

orchards from the main estate complex. It is situated close to the Le Rhône manor house (dated 1795) and a short walk from the winery. Here you can sit inside or out at wrought iron tables under a majestic old spreading oak. The seating area is flanked by two boules courts.

There are several eating options – the more formal Boschendal Restaurant (open seven days a week for lunch, booking essential) in the original Boschendal cellar offers a full Cape cuisine buffet, which has been serving dishes such as bobotie and desserts such as malva pudding for over 30 years. Le Café (open daily for brunch and lunch) housed in the old slave quarters, serves light meals and teas that can be enjoyed at tables under shady oaks. Le Pique Nique (daily in summer, weather permitting; booking essential) provides French-style picnic fare in wicker baskets, and dessert and coffee from Le Pavillon, the famous gazebo on the lawn where visitors picnic under the umbrellas and fragrant pines. Boschendal was the first estate in the winelands to provide picnics and these remain popular – reservations are essential, both for the picnics and the main restaurant.

CAPE CHAMONIX FARM

ADDRESS Uitkyk Street, Franschhoek

GPS S 33° 58' 23.3" E 18° 50' 51.0"

TEL +27 (0)21 876 8400

WEBSITE www.chamonix.co.za

TASTING & SALES Mon–Sat 09h30–16h30; Sun 09h30–16h00 (closed 25 Dec & 1 Jan)

AESTHETIC Tasting room in a quaint but unassuming old blacksmith's cottage up a Franschhoek side street downplays its status as being among the top handful of South African producers

ATTRACTIONS Marco Polo Lodge and various fully equipped self-catering cottages; private game reserve (for guests only); cellar tours (by appointment)

MUST DO Book a cellar tour – steep stairs from the tasting room take you down to a cobwebbed tunnel lined with riddling boards and bottles, and leading down into the underground cellar

MUST TASTE The Reserve Pinot Noir (but the wines are consistently good across the ranges, varietals and styles, so be guided by your own palate and preferences)

"As purists we have always believed that to produce a wine of true character, it is essential that nature be the primary winemaker." Gottfried Mocke, winemaker

Cape Chamonix is situated high on the eastern slopes of the Franschhoek valley. This working wine farm with its water-bottling plant (the water is sourced from crystal-clear underground springs deep within the mountains) has a history stretching back nearly 350 years.

It was originally part of 290-hectare La Cotte, one of the very first farms granted to the French Huguenots in 1688. The main homestead was built by Judge Malan in 1947. The farm was owned by the Pickering family from 1965 to 1988 and during this time its name was changed from Waterval (Waterfall) to Chamonix, which held memories for the family of a holiday they spent in France and is in keeping with its location in this Gallic corner of the winelands.

The estate was bought in 1991 by German-born Chris Hellinger, an avid art collector and game hunter. He set about making significant improvements, and planting new vines and fruit trees. He acquired Uitkyk, a small neighbouring farm, a few years later and an underground wine cellar, connected to the tasting room via a tunnel, was built. The tunnel's walls are lined with riddling racks filled with bottles of Méthode Cap Classique undergoing a second fermentation.

Today, Chamonix has 50 hectares under vineyard and boasts some of the highest-planted vines in the Cape winelands. These higher vineyards benefit from later sun in the morning and cooler temperatures in the afternoon.

In the decade-plus since Gottfried Mocke took charge of both vineyards and winemaking, he has focused on producing a premium range of site-specific wines that show their true character and individuality. An "almost unprecedented growth in quality" saw it chosen as Platter's South African Wine Guide Winery of the Year 2013.

Both the Reserve and the Cape Chamonix ranges offer wines of excellent quality. The Reserve range comprises the highly acclaimed Pinot Noir Reserve, Troika, which is a red blend, the Chardonnay Reserve, Sauvignon Blanc Reserve and the Reserve White. The Cape Chamonix range includes a Cabernet Sauvignon, the Greywacke Pinotage, a Chardonnay, Sauvignon Blanc and MCC Blanc de Blancs, as well as a red and a white blend.

The tasting centre is in the converted 'The Blacksmith's Cottage', which was built in the late Eighteenth century and has antique saddles and other equine memorabilia displayed on the walls. Also on offer for tasting is a range of grappa and schnapps from Chamonix's own distillery.

Just a bit further down from the tasting centre on the opposite side of the road, wrought-iron gates lead up to Chamonix estate with its guest accommodation in the safari-style Marco Polo Lodge and several self-catering options, from the Forest Suites and Waterfall Lodge to the various one- and two-bedroom cottages. A 50-hectare game farm (not open to the public) where guests can view bontebok, eland, ostrich, springbok and zebra, was developed by the owner, who is a nature enthusiast.

GRANDE PROVENCE HERITAGE WINE ESTATE

ADDRESS Main Road (R45), Franschhoek

GPS S 33° 53' 57.6" E 19° 06' 10.5"

TEL +27 (0)21 876 8600

WEBSITE: www.grandeprovence.co.za

TASTING & SALES Mon – Sat 10h00 – 18h00 (Apr – Oct), 10h00 – 19h00 (Nov – Mar); Sun 10h00 – 18h00 (closed on certain public holidays)

AESTHETIC Sophisticated; stylishly blends Cape Dutch architecture with classic French accents, reflecting its Huguenot heritage, and décor elements that root it intrinsically on the African continent

ATTRACTIONS The Restaurant; five-star The Owner's Cottage at Grande Provence; La Provençale B&B; The Shop; The Gallery, The Project Room and The Sculpture Garden; group tastings in The Cathedral, an extension of the art gallery (up to 120 people), and private tastings (up to 12 people) – both options to be pre-booked; cellar tours (Mon – Fri 11h00 & 15h00; other times or Sat/Sun by appointment)

MUST DO Visit the art gallery – an expert curator keeps the experience dynamic

MUST TASTE Shiraz, the best seller in the tasting room

Grande Provence Heritage Wine Estate lives up to its name, wearing its 300-year-old history with grace and gravitas. This well thought out tourism destination offers fine dining and wines, some of the best art in the country and luxury accommodation, all set in manicured gardens with immaculate hedges, 300-year-old oak trees and several soothing water features.

The first owner of this land more than three centuries ago was French Protestant Pierre Joubert, who fled his home town of La Motte-d'Aigues in Provence to avoid religious persecution. In 1694 he arrived in what was then named Olifantshoek (Elephants Corner). His family prospered and soon acquired other local farms, including La Motte (see page 72). These French beginnings are still reflected in the estate today.

In 2004, the property was purchased by a Dutch and Belgian consortium, making Grande Provence part of the elite Huka Retreats portfolio, which includes sister properties Huka Lodge in New Zealand, consistently rated one of the best in the world, and privately owned Dolphin Island in Fiji. The Huka Retreats are the vision of Dutch-born entrepreneur and Honorary Consul Alex van Heeren, who resides on the estate. New Zealand-based interior designer Virginia Fisher consults to the group and her assured sense of style is evident throughout the estate, from the restaurant and adjoining tasting room to the five-star accommodation, The Owner's Cottage, which is superbly appointed for indulgent contemporary comfort and features discreetly housed technology. La Provençale is a stylish cottage that accommodates up to four guests on a bed-and-breakfast basis.

There are 54 hectares of vineyards planted to noble varieties framing the driveway into the estate. The Grande Provence, a red blend, is the estate's flagship, and the range includes a Chardonnay, Chenin Blanc-Viognier, Sauvignon Blanc, Cabernet Sauvignon, Pinot Noir and Shiraz; a maiden Cap Classique has also been added. The popular entry-level Angels Tears collection of wines is available for purchase at cellar-door prices, but not for tasting.

The wine-tasting area leads off The Restaurant. The striking counter is made of galvanised steel and the cleverly designed 'tractor seat' bar stools are surprisingly comfy. Upholstered chairs in front of a fireplace invite guests to relax, sit back and enjoy their tasting experience. On summer days, wines can be tasted at the outside tables (except when the restaurant is fully booked). Imported French cheeses are available for enjoying with the wines and various tasting options include the Tastes of Grande Provence, designed by the winemaker and executive chef to afford visitors a chance to experience 'tastes' of dishes on the menu at The Restaurant.

The modern restaurant (open for lunch and dinner daily) features galvanised metal, steel joinery, skylights and a generous fireplace. Seating is at steel tables in white leather high-back chairs in the central row or blue chairs on either side. French doors open onto the courtyard with outdoor seating next to a pond for summer's days. Inside, fresh seasonal ingredients are skilfully prepared using classical French and innovative fusion influences, and are imaginatively presented. The Jonkershuis, with its distinctive chandeliers made from recycled wine bottles, caters for intimate private dining experiences.

The Gallery at Grande Provence (open daily) has established itself as a leading location for contemporary South African art, and features all the visual art forms, from painting to ceramics and sculpture. Expertly curated exhibitions change on a regular basis.

LA MOTTE

A culture of excellence is the ethos that drives this Franschhoek estate. Its exceptional tourism offering encompasses the finer things in life, from cuisine and culture to history, nature and, of course, wine. From the moment you turn into the gates, meticulous attention to detail is evident and this is carried right through each and every single facet of this winelands destination, which was named the South African winner of Best of Wine Tourism under the auspices of Great Wine Capitals of the World (GWC) in 2013 for the second consecutive year.

As you reach a bend in the driveway, you will see an imposing four-metre bronze sculpture, The Wine Bearer, by Knysna-based artist Toby Megan. Her overflowing goblet symbolises sharing and abundance, which sums up the experience you are about to enjoy.

La Motte is owned by Hanneli Rupert-Koegelenberg and managed by her husband, CEO Hein Koegelenberg, backed by a team of dedicated staff. The property was acquired in 1970 by her father, the late Dr Anton Rupert, an internationally respected businessman and conservationist. He and his wife Huberte were both avid art lovers and patrons. Hanneli is one of South Africa's leading mezzo-sopranos and an acclaimed Lieder recitalist under her professional name, Hanneli Rupert; music is an intrinsic part of the culture at La Motte, where monthly classical music concerts are presented in the historic cellar.

In 2010, La Motte started an extensive development programme called 'La Motte Redefined', which included revamping the landscape and constructing new venues, among them a tasting room, restaurant, museum and traditional farm shop, all the while keeping in mind the estate's rich French and Cape Dutch heritage.

La Motte's Historic Walk, conducted by an informative guide, proceeds through the magnificent rose gardens to take in the heritage buildings dating from 1751, of which four are provincial (previously known as national) monuments. Look out for the water mill, the oldest in working order in the valley, which produces the stone-ground flour used in the restaurant. The walk sets off from the museum, where you can learn about the estate's rich cultural history as well as the Rupert family, admire the impressive collection of famous South African artist JH Pierneef's work and also view a rotating selection of contemporary art by other distinguished artists.

La Motte took the first place in the category for Sustainable Wine Tourism Practices in the Great Wine Capitals of the World Best of Wine Tourism Awards for 2013. This WWF-SA Biodiversity & Wine Initiative Champion's

focus is on conserving and protecting hectares of natural habitat on the Wemmershoek Mountain. The farm now grows rare flower species, including disas and blushing brides. An ethereal oil operation produces flavours and fragrances from various plants, including lavender, buchu and Cape snow bush, for use in a range of body products, as well as food.

Another conservation-conscious project is a mountainside Hiking Trail where nature lovers can experience the estate's abundant birdlife, a wealth of indigenous flora and fauna, a protea garden and breathtaking views of the famous Franschhoek valley. As a recent addition to La Motte's other green initiatives, an Organic Walk takes visitors on a guided walk through the sustainably farmed and organically grown vineyards and the indigenous landscaped and protea gardens, ending at the biodynamic vegetable and herb garden that supplies the restaurant and farm shop with fresh produce. The walk concludes with a wine tasting.

At the well-stocked Farm Shop you can buy everything from freshly baked bread to seasonal produce and flowers, as well as specially selected gift items (including the range of Arômes de La Motte body products made from essential oils harvested on the estate), preserves, proteas, linen and other specially selected household items.

The first 4 000 vines were planted in 1752. Today, La Motte's 75 hectares of vineyard are farmed organically using advanced practices and the latest technology. La Motte's award-winning wines have earned an enviable reputation and are consistently excellent across the ranges. The wine portfolio comprises the La Motte collection; the Classic Collection; the premium Pierneef Collection; and the flagship Hanneli R, a Shiraz-based blend that is produced only in exceptional vintages.

The spacious and inviting tasting facility is staffed by friendly, well-informed 'wine ambassadors'. There's a large fireplace for cosy winter tastings. Wines can be sampled at the tasting counter, at long tasting tables or comfortably seated on sofas. You can also take a walk through the glass-doored barrel-filled maturation room.

La Motte's tutored Food and Wine Tasting, presented in the Shiraz Studio, a private room off the tasting room, pairs five La Motte wines with five tasting portions of Pierneef à La Motte's cuisine (Fridays 10h00, prior reservation essential).

Stylish and sumptuous, the Pierneef à La Motte Restaurant has some playful décor elements, such as custom-designed chandeliers made of dangling blue-and-white porcelain which tinkle like wind chimes in the breeze, and prints of Pierneef, to whom the restaurant pays homage, on the backs of the chairs at the open kitchen's countertop, which looks out onto a more informal café-style courtyard. There's an elegant more formal inside eating area that flows out onto the water deck, which fronts onto a pond, and a conservatory terrace with garden views (open for breakfast on Saturday and Sunday; lunch Tuesday to Saturday; dinner Thursday to Saturday; closed on Good Friday and Christmas Day).

Chef Chris Erasmus interprets traditional Cape winelands cuisine in a fresh, modern way, incorporating seasonal produce from the estate's vegetable garden – much of it grown from heirloom seeds – into dishes such as the signature Cape *bokkom* (salted dried fish) salad. A chalkboard of the day lists lunchtime options.

MAISON

ADDRESS Main Road (R45), Franschhoek

GPS S 33° 53' 09.7" E 19° 04' 39.8"

TEL +27 (0)21 876 2116

WEBSITE www.maisonestate.co.za

TASTING & SALES Apr – Jun & Aug – Nov:
Wed – Sun 10h00 – 17h00; Dec – Mar:
Tues – Sun 10h00 – 17h00 (closed 25 Dec)

AESTHETIC Celebrates the good life in
effortless style, refreshing in its simplicity

ATTRACTIONS The Kitchen at Maison; Deli

MUST DO Kick off your shoes and sit at
one of the long outside tables admiring the
vineyard views with the lush grass under
your bare feet and the very tame indigenous
chickens pecking about on the lawns

MUST TASTE The Shiraz with Maison's
home-cured biltong and blue cheese (save
some to pair with the straw wine too)
and the Cape Ruby port-style wine with
a chocolate truffle

For wine lover Chris Weylandt, the owner of well-known designer furniture and homeware store Weylandts, producing his own range of wines at this wine, olive and fruit farm is the realisation of one of his lifelong dreams. Chris and Kim Smith, his life-partner and fellow-director of Weylandts, bought the farm in 2003 and the first wines were bottled in 2008.

Chris' concept of 'good living' is brought to life in the original 1920s farmhouse with its weathered tin roof, which has been expertly redesigned to house the tasting room, deli and restaurant. White screeded floors and lots of glass let in the light to create a bright interior showcasing furniture from the Weylandts stores. Raw wood tables and Punto chairs, inspired by Danish designer Hans Wegner, embody the natural organic farmhouse style seamlessly woven with contemporary design. Exposed wooden floorboards and leather couches in front of a fireplace create a cosy lounge area. Even the loos, housed in a converted container, are stylish.

There are 4,6 hectares of vineyard, eco-consciously overseen by Antwan Bondesio who also makes the wines in the compact, true-to-variety range. There's a Chardonnay, two Chenin Blancs, Viognier, Shiraz, a food-friendly Blanc de Noir (also from Shiraz), a Cape ruby port, a straw wine and the latest addition to the range, a Cap Classique made from 100 per cent Chardonnay. The production of the limited-release Chardonnay and Viognier is so small that the label is stamped with Antwan's thumbprint. The wines are available at the farm and also in the Weylandts' stores nationwide.

Wine tastings – at one of two tables beneath chandeliers designed by Chris and made from upcycled wine bottles, either inside or on the couches under the trees – are unhurried and guests are encouraged to linger over a bottle of wine, the evocative background music adding to the experience. Tastings are conducted in a personalised way, from the full house premium tasting to the introductory tasting, in which Shiraz is paired with their home-cured biltong and blue cheese, the Cape ruby port with dark chocolate and hazelnut truffles (save some of the blue cheese to have with the straw wine, a delicious combination).

Chef Arno Janse van Rensburg studied at the Institute of Culinary Arts in Stellenbosch and worked at several top restaurants, including Ginja and Myoga in Cape Town, before opening The Kitchen at Maison (open for lunch and late afternoon tapas from Wednesday to Sunday; dinner on Fridays and Saturdays in the summer months). The bistro-styled restaurant has an easy, relaxed atmosphere and overlooks the vineyards with outside seating at two long raw wood tables, one of which is bolted to a tree. Fresh produce is

the focus of his menu, which is small and changes with the seasons, making use of the fruit, vegetables and herbs from the farm itself. Starters include delicious salads and tempura prawns; there are choices such as pasta, line fish, Karoo lamb rack or Shanghai pork belly for mains, plumped out by tempting tapas such as pink salt and pepper squid or locally cured salmon trout, as well as daily specials on the blackboard. The food is served on rustic wooden boards.

Only house wines are on offer but these cover all bases; there are also craft beers, including chef Arno's The Following, a blonde honey ale. There's a refreshing branded lemonade in a clever re-usable glass bottle and the excellent coffee comes from Terbodore Coffee Roasters on the Goederust farm nearby.

Freshly harvested produce from the farm, from aubergines, lemons and satsumas to chillies and olives, is used to make the chutney, pickles, preserves, relishes and hand-pressed extra virgin olive oil you'll find lining the deli shelves. There's also biltong, *droëwors*, *saucisson*, free-range eggs and breads.

FRANSCHHOEK MOTOR MUSEUM

The Franschhoek Motor Museum is located at L'Ormarins wine estate, which belongs to Johann Rupert, a member of one of the country's foremost business and wine dynasties. The museum offers visitors a chance to look back at more than 100 years of motoring. Its unique collection of motor vehicles, from Bugattis to Jaguars, Mercedes-Benz and Porsches, motorcycles, bicycles and motoring memorabilia exceeds 220, and ranges from an 1898 Beeston to a 2003 Ferrari Enzo supercar. This unique collection is presented in chronological order in four dehumidified halls. More than 80 exhibits are on display at any given time and themes change regularly. The museum is open Monday to Friday 10h00 – 17h00 (last admittance 16h00); Saturday and Sunday 10h00 – 16h00 (last admittance 15h00) and most public holidays (phone 021 874 9000 for confirmation). **www.fmm.co.za**

MÔRESON

ADDRESS Happy Valley Road, Franschhoek

GPS S 33° 53' 11.9" E 19° 03' 30.6"

TEL +27 (0)21 876 3055

WEBSITE www.moreson.co.za

TASTING & SALES Daily 09:30 – 17:00
(closed 25 Dec)

AESTHETIC Wonderfully quirky and
individual, focused passion underpins this
small farm where a contagious sense of
playfulness and fun pervades

ATTRACTIONS Bread & Wine Restaurant;
The Farm Grocer (charcuterie produced
by Neil Jewell for purchase); Exotic Plant
Company (exquisite orchids); bread-
making, charcuterie and wine-blending
classes (book well in advance); cellar tours

MUST DO Meet Miss Molly, the
Weimaranar depicted on the eponymous
range's labels (but be warned she can
be elusive); say hello to Congo the cat,
usually found sleeping on a chair at the
deli counter or sneaking a sip of cold water
from an ice bucket on a summer's day

MUST TASTE Premium Chardonnay; also
red blend Mata Mata

"Come and take a breather and indulge in what we believe makes life worth living – fabulous company, delectable food and delicious wine."

The address gives you an inkling of the experience that lies ahead: Môreson (which means morning sun) is aptly located at the end of the Happy Valley Road and it's exactly as it's described on their website – a little slice of magic. Turn into the farm with its vines and lemon trees and, even if it's your first visit, you'll be greeted like an old friend and soon be made to feel right at home.

It's a very relaxing place to while away an afternoon. A good place to start is at the tasting room if you're lunching here as only Môreson's wines are served at the Mediterranean-style Bread & Wine Vineyard Restaurant (open daily for lunch). The knowledgeable staff members present a very informative and entertaining tasting complete with humorous banter. On sunny days you can taste the wines on the terrace. There's a strong focus on Chardonnay and the Môreson range features several Méthode Cap Classiques, single-varietal bottlings and a Bordeaux-style red blend, Mata Mata.

Môreson is owned by US-based Richard Friedman whose daughter Nikki manages the farm. Also a part of the family stable is Le Quartier Français, an award-winning boutique hotel in the village of Franschhoek owned by Richard's sister Susan Huxter.

Spend some time on the farm and you'll soon realise that they're as passionate about their animals as their wine. They support a number of animal-related charities, and a portion of the proceeds from each bottle of Miss Molly wine sold goes to The South African Guide Dogs Association for the Blind and Animals in Distress. The popular range is named after their much-loved Weimaraner and she features on the labels of wines with wonderful names like In My Bed Cabernet Sauvignon-Merlot and Kitchen Thief Sauvignon Blanc.

For a wine tasting with a difference, you can sample a range of Môreson wines each individually paired with Neil Jewell's highly sought-after charcuterie at The Farm Grocer. UK-born Neil is very skilled at curing meat and uses only pasture-raised pigs from Glen Oakes farm in the Hemel-en-Aarde valley.

The menu at the eatery, which has lovely outdoor seating under umbrellas or, on colder days, inside the restaurant with its colourful and quirky interior, is fairly concise but offers delicious options such as soups, pastas and risottos,

all made using the very best ingredients. Neil's vivacious wife Tina manages the front of house and ensures that service levels are as good as the food. And the nice part is that you can stock up on Neil's charcuterie, which includes home-cured bacon and lamb ham, plus homemade preserves and breads at the Farm Grocer on your way out.

You could also sign up for a two-day charcuterie workshop with Neil or a bread-baking course with Tina (dates are available on the website; you need to book well in advance as they fill up fast). There's a wine-blending course that includes a private cellar tour and tasting from the tanks and barrels too, and if you're around during the crush there's the Blessing of the Harvest where you can learn how to make wine in the traditional way, from hand-picking the grapes to foot-stomping them to extract the juice. You also get to design your own label and collect your wine a few months later.

SOLMS-DELTA

ADDRESS Delta Road, off the Main Road
(R45), Franschhoek
GPS S 33° 51′ 49″ E 18° 59′ 25″
TEL +27 (0)21 874 3937
WEBSITE www.solms-delta.co.za
TASTING & SALES Daily 09h00 – 17h00
(closed 25 Dec & 1 Jan)
AESTHETIC Past, present and future
intertwine through the telling of
yesterday's forgotten stories, giving voice
to today's and transforming tomorrow's
ATTRACTIONS Fyndraai Restaurant;
Museum van de Caab and archaeological
sites; summer music concerts; walking farm
tours; Dik Delta indigenous fynbos culinary
garden; cellar tours (by appointment)
MUST DO Visit the museum, which offers
an emotive look into the lives of slaves on
wine farms in the early days at the Cape
MUST TASTE The unusual vine-dried wines

Solms-Delta bills itself as 'a farm with a difference' and, right from the start, this farm set out to do things differently, from the ownership structure to the wines, cuisine and cultural investment. Solms-Delta was the regional winner in the Innovative Wine Tourism Experiences at the 2012 Great Wine Capitals Best of Tourism Awards.

The property is made up of three adjoining farms – Lubeck, owned by Richard Astor, Delta, owned by Professor Mark Solms, and Deltameer, owned by the Wijn de Caab Trust, the beneficiaries of which are employees and residents with a 33 per cent equity stake in Solms Delta Pty Ltd. It's not just on paper that the beneficiaries (employees and residents) are wealthier – there's a strong sense of belonging and involvement in the farm, and bringing out the best in everyone with skills training and mentoring.

Co-owner and world-respected neuroscientist Mark Solms was the guiding hand behind the combination of culture, heritage, history and wine that brings some 30 000 visitors to this unique farm each year.

The best place to start is at the Museum van de Caab where you can explore the story of Delta farm and its people. A record of the social history of the 323-year-old farm is housed in the original wine cellar, which dates back to 1740. It's near a fairly recently excavated Later Stone Age settlement site and the exposed foundations of a 1670s hunting lodge, one of the oldest buildings in the Cape. The museum's name, which means 'from the Cape', honours the slave heritage and fascinating displays focus on the people who lived and worked on the farm, from pre-colonial to present times. One of the walls is covered by 200 stone plaques, each one commemorating a life given to the farm through slavery. The farm's story is told through the real voices of individual people, making for a unique and profoundly moving experience.

Since 2007, the Delta Trust has been funding ongoing research on the vernacular music of the Cape, which is showcased in a musical heritage centre next to the restaurant on the farm. Solms-Delta has its own band, Delta Optel, which plays a range of traditional favourites, as well as a brass band, marching minstrels and the Soetstemme ladies choir. Co-owners Richard Astor and Mark Solms were also the forces behind an annual Cape rural musical festival, inaugurated in April 2008, the Franschhoek Oesfees (harvest festival).

There are two ranges of wines – the top-tier Solms-Delta range features six wines including a rare-in-the-Cape desiccated Shiraz, Africana; Hiervandaan, a vine-dried Rhône-style blend, and Gemoedsrus, a port made from vine-dried

Candace's daughter
Pholida van de Kaap
Born 8.7.1818
Died 8.2.1819

Francina van de Kaap
Born circa 1788
Housemaid

Hanna van de Kaap
Born circa 1793
Housemaid

*"Solms-Delta wines
are the products of
a long and complex
struggle embodying the
aspirations and sacrifices
of innumerable ordinary
people, past and present."*

Shiraz. The Solms Astor range alludes to the Cape musical heritage – Langarm, Vastrap and Cape Jazz Shiraz.

Along with the conventional wine tasting experience, expertly conducted at tables under the trees or in a room adjacent to the main museum, there is also a multitude of special-interest guided tours to choose from (booking essential): Cape Music and Wine; Forest and River Walk and Wine; History, Archaeology and Wine; Social History and Wine; and the Vineyards, Cellar and Wine Tour.

Then there are tours tailor-made for foodies: the Cape Food and Wine Pairing, A Taste of our Food Heritage and the out-of-the-ordinary Dik Delta Food and Wine Pairing – each dish includes ingredients freshly picked from the Dik Delta Culinary Garden. This two-hectare garden, which is planted with indigenous edible plants (*veldkos*) like buchu and spekboom, is part of a larger 15-hectare fynbos renosterveld park, which the Dik Delta Culinary Gardens and Wine Walk takes you through.

The original Fyndraai restaurant, which features a glass floor that floats above the exposed foundations of the old wine cellar, now caters to tour groups and picnickers (open daily for lunch). Executive chef Shaun Schoeman and his team are now ensconced in the old stable building, renovated to house a well-equipped kitchen designed by him. He turned to his own Khoi roots and family heritage when he started the restaurant, by exploring the diverse culinary influences and tradition of the Cape, from Dutch and Indonesian to Khoisan.

The menu is a fusion of the *veldkos* of the indigenous Khoisan people, the Cape-Malay influences of the slaves, and South African cuisine or *boerekos*, which was developed by the European settlers at the Cape. The food is flavoured with indigenous herbs grown in the Dik Delta edible fynbos garden. In true Solms-Delta fashion, he started out with totally inexperienced kitchen staff whom he personally trained to be the top team they are today.

Book one of the very popular picnic baskets (September to April), freshly filled with delicious and unusual treats. A guide, who carries your basket and a blanket, will help you select a perfect spot on the lawn next to the forest, on the banks of the river or overlooking the dam (you're welcome to take a dip so bring your swimming gear). If you're in luck and it's available, you can get a fun ride there on the tractor-drawn trailer.

FRANSCHHOEK WINE TRAM

The new and unique Franschhoek Wine Tram, a world wine-tasting first, is owned by father-and-son team David and Sean Blyth who are fervent train enthusiasts. The design of the newly constructed tram was based on the open-sided Brill Trams of the 1890s. A green initiative, it utilises the latest in bio-diesel engine technology. The tram, which sports French flags, seats 32 passengers. Flip-over seat backs on six of the eight benches afford them views in both directions. The hop-on, hop-off tour is a combination of the tram and a tram-bus and links several of the top cellar doors in the valley. It operates daily from 10h00 to 15h20 and departs every 40 minutes. Tickets can be purchased at the Franschhoek Wine Tram office at Bijoux Square, 60 Huguenot Road or online at **www.winetram.co.za**.

Paarl

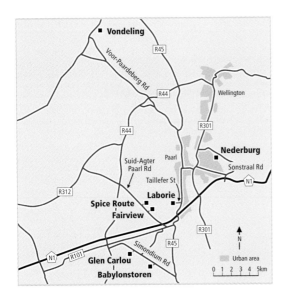

Also of interest

PAARL WINE ROUTE **www.paarlwine.co.za**

SCALI **www.scali.co.za**

REGION Coastal | **DISTRICT** Paarl

WARDS Simonsberg-Paarl; Voor Paardeberg

About 50 kilometres from Cape Town, the scenic town of Paarl is situated beneath the second-largest granite outcrop in the world. This is formed by three rounded domes, the most prominent of which is named Paarl Rock. Dutch bailiff Abraham Gabbema, who was despatched inland from the Cape in October 1659 on a trading expedition with the local Khoi tribes, set up camp next to a river below a majestic mountain. After it had rained, he looked up and saw the granite domes on the mountain gleaming and called them '*de Diamondt en de Peerlberg*' (the Diamond and Pearl Mountain) and that's how Paarl got its name.

In 1687, Cape Governor Simon van der Stel granted 21 farms along the Berg River to Dutch Free Burghers. These intrepid colonists were followed a year later, in 1688, by the first influx of French Protestant refugees who, having fled religious persecution in their homeland, were offered a safe haven in the Cape.

Paarl is South Africa's third-oldest European settlement. It's also the second-oldest wine route in the country and home to KWV, the first branded cellar in the country, as well as the world-renowned Nederburg Auction. Paarl's climate is typically Mediterranean and the Berg River flows through the length of the valley, supplying a natural source of irrigation. A large variety of grapes is grown in Paarl, including Chardonnay, Chenin Blanc, Cabernet Sauvignon, Pinotage and Shiraz, which have the best potential.

Paarl is also home to several olive farms and some of the most well-known brands of olive-related products in the country.

The district boasts a large area of unspoilt natural beauty and offers several outdoor activities.

BABYLONSTOREN

ADDRESS Simondium Road (R45),
Klapmuts, Paarl

GPS S 33° 49′ 21″ E 18° 55′ 48″

TEL +27 (0)21 863 3852

WEBSITE www.babylonstoren.com

TASTING & SALES Daily 10h00 – 16h00

AESTHETIC Pared-down style; a sense of
authenticity, integrity and providence

ATTRACTIONS Five-star Babylonstoren
Farm Hotel and Garden Spa; Babel
restaurant; Green House (light meals and
teas); deli; gift shop; guided garden tours
(daily 10h00, booking advised); hiking and
walking trails; hosted wine tasting with
cellar tour (to be pre-booked)

MUST DO A guided garden tour; visit with
each change of season to see nature at
work and don't miss the Clivia Walk

MUST TASTE Still early days but the Shiraz
and Babel, a merlot-led blend, stand out

One of the oldest Cape Dutch farms, this Seventeenth-century property just outside Paarl was a fruit farm until a decade ago when Karen Roos, a former interior magazine editor, acquired it and began the task of restoring it with the assistance of her team. Her assured touch is evident in the clean-lined contemporary aesthetic, which nonetheless reflects over 300 years of history and tradition. Centuries-old remnants of blue-patterned Delftware were found on the farm and these have been integrated into the branding, linking the farm to its past.

Today, Babylonstoren remains a working farm but the revitalised property also encompasses a five-star country getaway with a spa, Babel restaurant (open for lunch Wednesday to Sunday; dinner Friday and Saturday), the Green House tea room (open daily for light meals and teas), a winery, a tasting room and deli, as well as a shop selling produce from the farm. Visitors are encouraged to relax, explore the farm, and pick their own fruit and vegetables in the three-and-a-half hectare formal garden, which is the focal point of the farm. Inspired by the Company Gardens of the Dutch East India Company, the halfway stop between Europe and Asia where its ships once replenished their supplies on the long sea voyage, it was designed by renowned French landscape architect Patrice Taravella.

Diversity is a trademark of the garden, which features over 300 plant varieties, and everything planted in it is edible, medicinal or useful, and grown biologically. It was laid out on a grid, with 15 designated areas for fragrant indigenous plants, fruits, herbs and vegetables, beehives, chickens and ducks. A stream is gravity-fed into canals flowing through the garden for irrigation. There's a walled meditation garden, hanging woven 'nests' from which to view the birdlife, a prickly pear maze to wander through and the Clivia Walk along the river bank, which is spectacular when the clivias are in bloom in spring.

Babylonstoren has a well-preserved *werf* (farmyard), comprising the H-shaped manor house, original old cellar, *koornhuis* (where hay and wheat were once stored), a bell tower, a row of old stables and workshops, a fowl pen and a dovecote surrounded by whitewashed walls. Some of the old buildings were converted into guest cottages and a disused old cowshed was turned into the restaurant, Babel. The more casual eatery, the Green House, is a conservatory under oak trees where exotic fruits and a baobab tree grow. Both restaurants follow a 'from-farm-to-table' ethic and the emphasis is on simply but expertly prepared fresh, seasonal fare. Artisanal products, from breads baked in the old wood-fired oven to charcuterie and farm cheeses, are on offer in the deli. There is also a gift shop selling farm produce. Fourteen

"Above all we would like visitors to ground themselves again."
Karen Roos, owner

whitewashed guest cottages, built to reflect the farm's colonial heritage, line an avenue of oaks. A spacious glass box, slotted into a wall of each suite, contains a dining and cooking area with views over the gardens or into the trees.

Wine was made on Babylonstoren centuries ago and for the last few decades the grapes from the farm's vineyards were sold to big, co-operative cellars. Recently Babylonstoren entered the wine market again with a well-equipped 300-ton winery and a barrel maturation cellar that have the same specific 'footprint' as the original cellar buildings, which are splayed at an angle to the manor house. All 11 grape varieties grown on the farm are showcased in a vineyard surrounding the whitewashed cellar. Informative cellar tours follow the winemaking process from vineyard to bottle. You can also visit the distillery, where fruit grown in the gardens is made into *mampoer* (fruit brandy).

Babylonstoren's first wines were made in 2011 and the range features the flagship Chardonnay and Shiraz, a Chenin Blanc, Mourvèdre Rosé, Viognier and Bordeaux-style red blend. Also available for tasting are specially selected wines from 29 nearby wineries, offering visitors the convenience of a regional tasting experience with the wines for purchase at cellar-door prices.

FAIRVIEW

ADDRESS Suid-Agter Paarl Road, Paarl

GPS S 33° 46' 19.16" E 18° 55' 25.26"

TEL +27 (0)21 863 2450

WEBSITE www.fairview.co.za

TASTING & SALES Daily 09h00 – 17h00
(closed on certain public holidays)

AESTHETIC Landmark goat tower presides
over comfortably rustic farmyard with a
Mediterranean feel

ATTRACTIONS The Goatshed restaurant;
bread market on Saturdays; farm produce
and Fairview cheeses; Junior Cheese
Masters in summer (where children learn
how to make cheese)

MUST DO A tutored master tasting; view
a visual history of the farm and its quirky
brands on the tasting room walls

MUST TASTE An extensive range with
many standouts, especially the Shiraz and
white blends; try the first Rhône-style
MCC in South Africa

"You can't get away with wine tastings only anymore. You have to create an overall experience for visitors."

Charles Back, owner

Brilliant wine marketer Charles Back, the owner of Fairview, has built successful brands such as the Goats do Roam Wine Company and the pioneering Spice Route Winery (see page 100), which put the Swartland on the map. Undoubtedly Fairview's best-known landmark is its distinctive six-metre-high goat tower. Built in 1981, it is home to a select few of the over 1 000 herd on the farm, which supplies milk for the on-site Vineyard Cheesery and was also the inspiration behind the Goats do Roam brand (the wines are made at Fairview and are available for tasting, as is the case with the La Capra range too).

Fairview, purchased by Lithuanian grandfather Charles in the late 1930s, is a third-generation family-owned farm, with a long-held reputation for hospitality that stretches back to the 1970s when Cyril and Beryl Back first welcomed guests to their property. Today, this relaxed and family-friendly wine farm is one of the most-visited venues in the winelands with some 250 000 feet through its doors annually.

The wine and cheese tasting room features a number of tasting pods, creating an informal environment in which to taste from the wide range available, which includes wines from the single-vineyard range. Your tasting also includes a selection of Fairview's Jersey and goat's milk cheeses, which you can choose in the deli. Special seated, tutored tastings conducted by highly qualified staff take place in the Beryl Back Master Tasting Room, named in honour of Charles' late mother (booking is recommended).

The popular Mediterranean-style eatery The Goatshed (open daily for breakfast and lunch) offers light meals and lunches, from cheese platters and fresh breads to salads and seasonal country fare, in what was once an old wine cellar and is now a relaxed and rustic setting. There's a terrace for alfresco eating too. You can choose a wine from the full portfolio to accompany your meal – there's also a selection available in 200 ml carafes.

GLEN CARLOU

ADDRESS Simondium Road, Klapmuts, Paarl

GPS S 33° 48′ 34.44″ E 18° 54′ 19.41″

TEL +27 (0)21 875 5528

WEBSITE www.glencarlou.co.za

TASTING & SALES Mon–Fri 08h30–17h00; Sat/Sun 10h00–16h00 (closed Good Friday & 25 Dec)

AESTHETIC The airy thatch-roofed tasting room and restaurant building would look as at home in the African bushveld as it does in the Cape winelands

ATTRACTIONS Glen Carlou Restaurant; Hess Art Collection Museum; cellar tours (by appointment)

MUST DO View the contemporary art collection for an overview of the most significant genres of the past four decades

MUST TASTE Gravel Quarry Cabernet Sauvignon and Quartz Stone Chardonnay, both from the Prestige range

"We consistently produce wines of integrity and quality."
Arco Laarsman, winemaker

Glen Carlou was established on the Simonsberg slopes in 1985 by the Finlaysons, a well-known Cape wine family, who built the farm's reputation for consistency and continuity. Since 2003, the 145-hectare farm with its 70 hectares of vineyards has been successfully owned and run by the Switzerland-based Hess Family Wine Estates.

The spacious open-plan visitor centre encompasses a lounge area with comfy couches, a curved mahogany tasting counter, a restaurant seating area (open daily for lunch; sundowner tapas on Thursday and Friday in summer; closed on certain public holidays) and panoramic Paarl valley and mountain views through floor-to-ceiling windows or from the marble terrace with its umbrella-shaded tables and chairs. A glass floor panel allows visitors to look down onto the wine barrels in the maturation cellar below.

Glen Carlou is known for its Chardonnays. These include an unwooded version, a small but growing category, which is vinified in an egg-shaped Nomblot concrete fermenter, an alternative to tanks or barrels, designed

by Frenchman Marc Nomblot. There is a Prestige, Reserve and Classic range as well as the affordable Tortoise Hill Red and White in the Tortoise Hill range. While visiting Glen Carlou, it's possible to sample international vintages from the Australian, Argentinian and Californian wineries in the Hess portfolio too.

Also, take the time to walk through the Hess Museum of Contemporary Art, an exhibition space adjacent to the lounge area of the visitor centre, which showcases a small but impressive selection from the more than 1 000 works in Donald Hess's collection, which he began accumulating as a young man.

'Custodians of the land, farming in harmony with nature,' is the Hess Family Wine Estates' philosophy. Glen Carlou is a member of the WWF-SA Biodiversity & Wine Initiative and follows sustainable farming principles such as conserving water, recycling waste water and using minimal herbicides and pesticides. The Zen fynbos garden with its magnificent array of endemic plants supports numerous small mammals and birds – over 60 species have been counted.

LABORIE WINE FARM

ADDRESS Taillefer Street (off Main Road), Paarl

GPS S 33° 45' 57.64" E 18° 57' 31.84"

TEL +27 (0)21 807 3390

WEBSITE www.laboriewines.co.za

TASTING & SALES Mon – Sat 09h00 – 17h00; Sun 11h00 – 17h00 (closed on certain public holidays)

AESTHETIC Historic Cape Dutch *werf* scenically situated between landmark Paarl Rock and the bustling main street

ATTRACTIONS Harvest Restaurant; Anglo Boer War monument; permanent Cecil Skotnes art exhibition; cellar tours (by appointment)

MUST DO A chocolate and wine pairing – the artisan chocolates are handmade by Chocolats Marionettes in Knysna and flavours include an unusual Milk Cape Malay Spice, which is paired with Shiraz; an olive and wine pairing

MUST TASTE Jean Taillefert Shiraz, if you like yours modern, spicy and generously oaked

This KWV-owned property is situated off the main road – a 12-kilometre stretch and the longest in South Africa. It showcases superb examples of Art Deco, Cape Dutch, Edwardian and Victorian architecture. The recently refurbished estate lies below Paarl Rock, which dramatically backdrops the vineyards clambering up the northern foothills of the mountain.

The farm was granted to Isaac Taillefert in 1691 and named after the district of La Bri in France, where this prosperous French Huguenot family came from. As he already owned the neighbouring farm, Picardie, he put the farm in his son Jean's name and they set about clearing the bush and planting the vines – not a task for the faint-hearted! Wine was produced seven years later in 1698, the same year that Frenchman François Lequat visited the Cape. He later wrote in his book, *A New Voyage to the East Indies* published in 1708, that their wine was "the best in the colony and similar to our small wines of Champagne". Today, the flagship Jean Taillefert Shiraz, a generously oaked spicy wine, honours this early owner.

KWV bought Laborie in 1972 and began turning it into a world-class estate. In 1977, the Manor House at Laborie, which was built in 1750 and is one of best examples of a Cape Dutch farm and *werf*, was proclaimed a national monument. The guesthouse has one room in this manor house and eight luxurious suites adjacent to it.

The Taillefert family, with their knowledge of French viticulture, laid a solid foundation for the vineyards. In recent years replanting has been a focus area, especially of Chardonnay, Pinot Noir and Pinot Meunier for the production of Laborie's Methode Cap Classique, Blanc de Blanc, Brut and Rosé.

Laborie's tasting room boasts a view of the Paarl valley and the Paarl and Drakenstein mountains, which you can take in from the balcony in the summer; in winter, there's a welcoming fire in this intimate venue.

Harvest at Laborie, headed up by acclaimed consulting chef Matthew Gordon, is a family-friendly restaurant with seating for 80 guests inside and 100 on the terrace under leafy oaks with vineyard and mountain views (open daily for lunch; dinner from Wednesday to Saturday). The work of one of South Africa's great artists, Cecil Skotnes, is exhibited at Laborie and can be viewed in the restaurant, tasting room and manor house.

Laborie, one of the first members of the WWF-SA Biodiversity & Wine Initiative, has demarcated ten per cent of the total farm area, including certain reclaimed mountainside vineyards, for fynbos regeneration. The farm borders on the Paarl Mountain Nature Reserve and the new fynbos areas have already attracted various species of flora and fauna.

NEDERBURG WINES

ADDRESS Sonstraal Road, Daljosafat, Paarl

GPS S 33° 43' 15.4" E 19° 0' 9.4"

TEL +27 (0)21 862 3104

WEBSITE www.nederburg.co.za

TASTING & SALES Mon – Fri 09h00 – 17h00;
Sat/Sun 10h00 – 16h00 (summer);
Sat 10h00 – 16h00 (winter); closed on
certain public holidays

AESTHETIC History and innovation
combine at this Paarl winery with its
rich winemaking past

ATTRACTIONS Historic manor house;
visitors' centre; The Red Table, a bistro-style
restaurant; cheese and wine platters, potstill
brandy, coffee and biscotti, picnics; cellar
tours Mon – Fri 10h30 & 15h00, Sat 11h00,
Sun 11h00 (Nov – Mar); annual summer
outdoor concert (see the website for details)

MUST DO Visit the Old Cellar museum with
its fascinating timeline covering over two
centuries of winemaking at Nederburg;
pop in to the cellar to see the ornate
carved barrels

MUST TASTE Ingenuity red and white
blends; noble late harvests: Edelkeur, the
Cape's first Noble Late Harvest, and the
Winemaker's Reserve NLH

"Winemaking is an act enriched through experience."
Razvan Macici, cellarmaster

There's always something new happening at this gracious historic winery set against the dramatic Drakenstein mountains on the outskirts of Paarl, from being the location for the filming of television series *MasterChef South Africa* to turning the manor house into an eatery with tables spilling out into the gardens. Innovations aside, the core of Nederburg remains its wines – an extensive but well-constructed range and an unparalleled award-winning track record in recent years make the tasting complex central to the winery.

One of South Africa's best-known brands, Nederburg has a broad range of wines available for tasting in the stylish tasting centre. There are several tiers in the range to suit a variety of palates and pockets – 56Hundred, Foundation, Winemaster's Reserve, Heritage Heroes, Manor House and Ingenuity – as well as special-edition wines (when available) and the alembic solera brandy. The wines for the Nederburg Auction are labelled as Private Bin.

The annual wine auction that Nederburg hosts has become one of the top wine auctions in the world and serves as a valuable showcase for South African wines, including rare and speciality bottlings. This event also raises funds for the Nederburg Charity Trust with its various beneficiaries.

Nederburg has a rich heritage stretching back over two centuries. The Heritage Heroes range of wines honours the personalities who played a major part in Nederburg's history and made it what it is today. For example, the Anchorman, pays tribute to the first owner, Philippus Wolvaart, who acquired the farm in 1791.

In 1800, Wolvaart completed the beautifully proportioned thatch-roofed Cape Dutch manor house, which features yellowwood shutters, beams and doors, Batavian floor tiles and one of the loveliest gables of its type. It was a remarkable feat as most of the building materials had to be transported from Cape Town, which involved at least two days' journey by cart! The H-shaped homestead, built with sun-dried bricks bound with clay mortar, is now a national monument.

Today, top local and international classical musicians perform their concerts here during the annual Sunday night Nederburg Classic Concert Series, and the manor house also plays host to special events, and private or corporate lunches and dinners (by prior arrangement).

The property changed hands several times until it was purchased in 1937 by a German viticulturist, brewer and tea specialist, Johann Georg Graue, who meticulously managed the vineyards and revolutionised winemaking at Nederburg. A pioneer of new technology and techniques, he had a huge impact on the entire South African wine industry. Günter Brözel, the legendary cellarmaster from 1956 to 1989, took Nederburg to new heights and today Nederburg's current cellarmaster, Razvan Macici, continues this legacy.

SPICE ROUTE WINERY

"The vision for Spice Route is to offer local and international tourists a group of hand-picked artisanal producers who put as much thought, skill and passion into their products as the Spice Route winemaker, Charl du Plessis, does when crafting his wines."

Charles Back, owner

ADDRESS Suid-Agter Paarl Road, Paarl
GPS S 33° 45' 50.5" E 18° 55' 9.7"
TEL +27 (0)21 863 5200
WEBSITE www.spiceroutewines.co.za
TASTING & SALES Daily 09h00 – 17h00 (closed on certain public holidays)
AESTHETIC On the mountainside with sweeping views from the shady terrace; décor elements reminiscent of Zanzibar emphasise the Spice Route theme
ATTRACTIONS Spice Route Restaurant; Tasting Room; Barley & Biltong Emporium beer garden; Cape Brewing Company; Red Hot Glass glass-blowing studio; DV Artisan Chocolate; Wilderer's Distillery & La Grapparia Restaurant
MUST DO Visit the micro beer brewery, grappa distillery and chocolate factory to see the producers in action; try a delicious chocolate and wine pairing or a food and wine pairing
MUST TASTE Chenin Blanc (which goes well with spicy food) and Syrah; also try the Mourvèdre, one of only a dozen or so produced in the Cape

When Charles Back, wine industry visionary and owner of Fairview (see page 92), acquired the farm Klein Amoskuil in 1997, it was a catalyst for a resurgence of winegrowing in the Swartland. The revival was led by some of the country's most talented young winemakers, who are now grouped under the Swartland Revolution banner (see page 29).

For a long time Spice Route was a wine brand without a 'home' but that changed with the purchase of the farm next door to Fairview in Paarl. Now this wine brand, previously only available for tasting at Fairview, has found a home that offers a wonderful destination for the whole family and encompasses several visitor experiences on one property, from a micro-brewery to a chocolatier and a grappa distillery.

The brand name reflects the Cape's origins as a refreshment station for ships plying the Spice Route to bring the flavoursome spices of the East back to Europe. It also evokes the rich, complex style of wines in the range with exotic names such as Chakalaka and Malabar. Spice Route's award-winning wines can be tasted in the underground tasting room, part of the old cellar on the farm, or outside under the pergola or even lazing on the lawn.

The Spice Route tasting room offers three wine tasting 'Journeys': the Wine Journey, a standard tasting of a selection of six wines, including the flagship Malabar and Syrah; the Wine and Chocolate Journey, which pairs six Spice Route wines with four DV Artisan chocolates; and the Food and Wine Journey, which allows you to taste seven wines from the range and includes five food pairings prepared by the Spice Route Restaurant's chefs.

The Spice Route Restaurant (open daily for lunch, with extended hours for sundowner dinners on Friday and Saturday in summer) explores the fusion between spice, food and wine, from traditional South African cooking to culinary influences along the Spice Route from Europe to the East. Head chef Marion Kumpf has created her own Spice Route Deli Range of spice

grinders and condiments, which are available for purchase at the restaurant.

Artisanal products, from chocolate to hand-blown glass, are made on the premises by passionate craftsmen, making for a fun and educational experience. Red Hot Glass is one of very few Venetian-style molten glass-blowing studios in South Africa and here you can watch artist Liz Lacey in action. The De Villiers family's DV Artisan Chocolate is one of a handful of 'bean to bar' micro batch chocolatiers in the world. At the Cape Brewery Company (CBC), highly skilled brewmaster Wolfgang Koedel produces a wide range of beers that can be tasted either on tap or bottled at the Barley & Biltong Emporium beer garden, which serves a selection of beer paired with beef, kudu and springbok biltong. The Wilderer's Distillery is where master distiller Helmut Wilderer crafts internationally acclaimed grappa and *eau de vie* (schnapps). Visitors can view the distillation process and sample some of the products. Wood-fired thin-based pizzas, *flammküchen* and tapas served with a glass of grappa or schnapps are available at the La Grapparia Restaurant next door.

VONDELING

ADDRESS Voor-Paardeberg Road,
Agter Paarl

GPS S 33° 37' 27" E 18° 51' 65"

TEL +27 (0)21 869 8339

WEBSITE www.vondelingwines.co.za

TASTING & SALES Mon–Fri 10h00–17h00;
Sat by appointment only (closed on certain
public holidays unless by prior arrangement)

AESTHETIC Vineyards and fynbos cover
these slopes of the Paardeberg, a
distinctive rocky granite outcrop best
viewed from the generous *stoep* at the
thatched tasting facility

ATTRACTIONS Light, picnic-style lunches
available and Sunday lunches (booking
essential, see website for dates); cellar
tours and guided seasonal tours (both by
appointment only)

MUST DO Book a tour of the atmospheric
cellar or the fynbos-covered mountainside

MUST TASTE Babiana, a white blend, and
the Erica Shiraz are the stars of the show

The farms in the unspoilt rural Voor-Paardeberg ward surround a granite outcrop, the Paardeberg. Vondeling is one of the few wineries in the area that is open to the public – the others are by appointment only so if you plan ahead you could book a tasting at nearby Scali.

On the southern summit there's an Eighteenth-century VOC signal cannon that reflects Vondeling's long history. The farm was granted to Swedish immigrant Oloff Bergh in 1704 and the original farm house, now restored and turned into a luxurious guesthouse comprising seven en-suite bedrooms, dates back to 1750. It is set in peaceful gardens with shaded terraces, a 20-metre swimming pool, barbecue area and spotlit tennis court.

Englishman Julian Johnsen, the managing director and a co-owner together with two old childhood friends in the UK, Anthony Ward and Richard Gower, bought Vondeling in 2002. The neighbouring farm, Klein Vondeling, was added soon after that. In 2010, they bought St Clement, well-known golfer David Frost's farm just over the road from Vondeling's entrance. They revamped the tasting centre and terrace, which offer incredible views of the farm and over to the mountains beyond, and built a small steepled chapel for wedding ceremonies.

Vondeling has a three-centuries-old winemaking tradition dating back to the early 1700s. Today, minimal intervention during the vinification process ensures wines with a unique 'fingerprint' of origin. The winemaking operation is now housed in the large, modern cellar on St Clement farm and barrel maturation takes place in the atmospheric old cellar on Vondeling.

Julian nurtures the lands with their 100 hectares of vineyards and follows a 'biological' approach to farming these slopes, where cooling south-westerly winds blow in every afternoon from the Atlantic Ocean. There's a distinctly Mediterranean slant when it comes to more recent plantings and crop yields are low, ranging between six to eight tons per hectare.

Sustainability is coupled with a progressive approach. The various landowners who have mountain properties have formed the Paardeberg Conservancy, where cameras have captured images of Cape leopard and other smaller cats, as well as antelope, baboons and porcupines. A commendable project documenting fynbos was started after the raging fire in January 2011 destroyed 70 per cent of the 4000 hectares of Boland granite fynbos. The Paardeberg Sustainability Initiative, in conjunction with Vondeling, commissioned a fynbos survey. So far approximately 900 species in over 70 families have been collected and documented. Two of the wines, Vondeling Babiana and Erica Shiraz, have been named for two of the red-data listed plants that are endemic to this mountain: *Babiana noctiflora* and *Erica hippurus*. A new, as yet to be named, species was also discovered.

Stellenbosch

REGION COASTAL | **DISTRICT** STELLENBOSCH
WARDS BANGHOEK | BOTTELARY | DEVON VALLEY
JONKERSHOEK VALLEY | PAPEGAAIBERG | POLKADRAAI HILLS

The original Stellenbosch Wine Route was founded in 1971 and is the oldest in the country. The wine route turned a new page in 2002 with the founding of the Stellenbosch American Express® Wine Routes, which represents and promotes a co-ordinated network of some 150 wineries. It is one of the most popular tourist attractions in the Western Cape, visited annually by tourists from all around the world.

Situated in the broad and fertile valley of the Eerste River (First River), Stellenbosch is the second-oldest winemaking centre in South Africa next to Constantia. At its hub lies Stellenbosch, the town of oaks, which features some of the finest examples of Cape Dutch architecture. Located about an hour's drive east of Cape Town, the town still retains the open irrigation canals that were planned in the Seventeenth century by Simon van der Stel, after whom the settlement took its name. Winemaking was an integral part of this pioneer community's culture and life from the outset, as it is today. Stellenbosch, with its blend of centuries-old estates and contemporary wineries, includes some of the most well-known names in Cape wine.

Stellenbosch is the educational and research centre of the winelands. Stellenbosch University is the only university in South Africa that offers a degree in viticulture and oenology, and many of the country's most successful winemakers studied here, or at the Elsenburg School of Agriculture, just outside the town. Also on the outskirts of Stellenbosch is the ARC Infruitec-Nietvoorbij Institute for Viticulture and Oenology, which

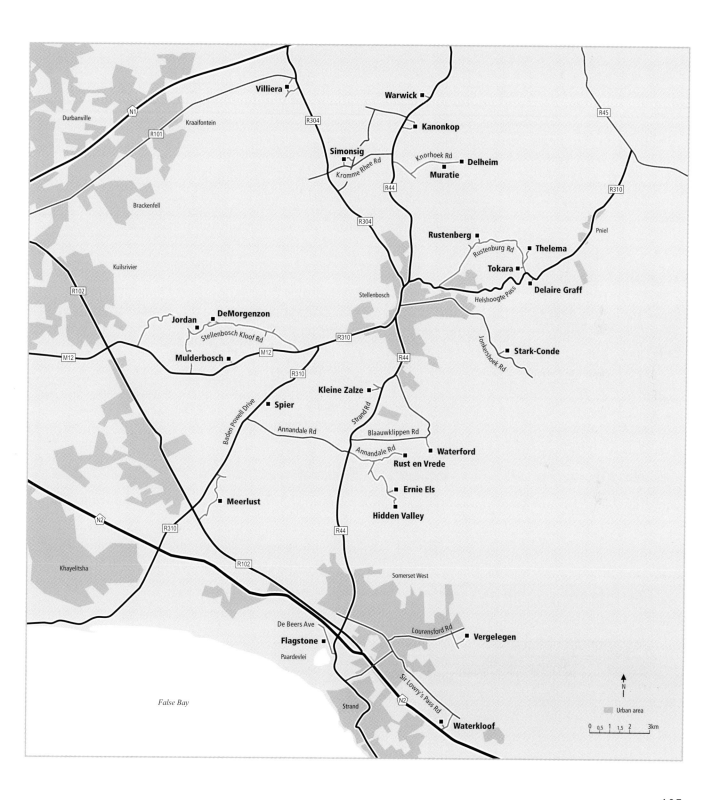

Durbanville

N1

Kraaifontein

R101

Brackenfell

Kuilsrivier

R102

M12

M12

Khayelitsha

N2

R310

R102

False Bay

Villiera ■

R304

Warwick ■

Kanonkop ■

R45

Simonsig ■

Knorhoek Rd

Delheim ■

Kromme Rhee Rd

Muratie ■

R44

R304

Rustenberg ■

Thelema ■

Rustenburg Rd

Tokara ■

R310

Pniel

Stellenbosch

Delaire Graff ■

Helshoogte Pass

Jordan ■

DeMorgenzon ■

Stellenbosch Kloof Rd

R310

Jonkershoek Rd

Stark-Conde ■

Mulderbosch ■

R44

Baden Powell Drive

R310

Kleine Zalze ■

Spier ■

Strand Rd

Annandale Rd

Blaauwklippen Rd

Annandale Rd

Waterford ■

Rust en Vrede ■

Ernie Els ■

Meerlust ■

Hidden Valley ■

R44

N2

Somerset West

De Beers Ave

Lourensford Rd

Flagstone ■

Vergelegen ■

Paardevlei

Strand

Sir Lowry's Pass Rd

N2

Waterkloof ■

N

■ Urban area

0   0,5   1   1,5   2   3km

boasts one of the most modern experimental wineries in the world, and experimental farms situated in several winegrowing districts. The organisation undertakes important research into all aspects of viticulture and oenology.

The winegrowing area encompasses several mountain ranges – the Hottentots Holland, Helderberg, Stellenbosch and Simonsberg mountains. This mountainous terrain coupled with ample rainfall, deep well-drained soils and a diversity of terroirs make it a much sought-after viticultural area. The intensively farmed Stellenbosch district has been divided up into six distinct wards.

Conditions in this district are particularly well suited to the cultivation of many of the noble varieties. Almost all the noble wine grape varieties are produced here and the area is also known for the quality of its blended reds.

There are five manageable sub-routes for tourists, which each have their own characteristics in terms of wine styles, micro climates and geographical location: Bottelary Hills, Greater Simonsberg, Helderberg, Stellenbosch Berg and Stellenbosch Valley.

Also of interest **www.wineroute.co.za**

ARCHITECTURE

The Cape winelands are renowned both for their Cape Dutch architecture and contemporary design, with the most modern of wineries often juxtaposed against a centuries-old gabled manor house. The original homes of the first settlers at the Cape were generally modest. During the prosperous Eighteenth and Nineteenth centuries, farmers extended their homes, adding new wings as families and fortunes grew. This resulted in the classical H-shaped homestead. They typically adorned them with distinctive gables, which also had a practical purpose – the end-gables helped stop the strong winds at the Cape from ripping off the thatch. Historians also suggest that gables over doorways prevented burning thatch landing on fleeing occupants in the event of a fire.

Designed by Christoph Dornier, the loft-style winery at Dornier (opposite) is a fine example of innovative contemporary design. The sculptural curved-roof building of face-brick and reflecting materials mirrors the shape of the Stellenbosch Mountain behind it, and contrasts with the historic buildings on the farm.

DELAIRE GRAFF ESTATE

ADDRESS Helshoogte Pass (R310),
Stellenbosch

GPS S 33° 55′ 20.4″ E 18° 55′ 26.0″

TEL +27 (0)21 885 8160

WEBSITE www.delaire.co.za

TASTING & SALES Mon–Sat 10h00–17h00;
Sun 10h00–16h00 (closed on certain
public holidays)

AESTHETIC Opulent lifestyle destination
with meticulously maintained grounds and
gardens; art is the theme that connects these
stimulating spaces, both indoors and out

ATTRACTIONS Delaire Graff and Indochine
restaurants; five-star Lodge and Spa; Graff
Diamonds Store; 100% Capri Boutique; art
collection; cellar tours (by appointment)

MUST DO View the acclaimed collection
of South African artworks

MUST TASTE The age-worthy Chardonnay,
the Sauvignon Blancs and Botmaskop, a
Cabernet-led blend

"Delaire aims for red wines that are big in structure, with soft tannins and elegance, while the white wines must capture the freshness of the harvest."

Morné Vrey, winemaker

On landing at the Cape in 1688, the French Huguenots faced a perilous crossing over the mountain pass to the remote valley wherein they had been allocated farms by the Dutch East India Company. Delaire Graff Estate's high-altitude vineyards lie on the slopes of Botmaskop, which was originally named Bootmanskop (meaning Boatman's Peak) and was once used as a lookout point for ships entering the harbour at Table Bay. A sentry would alert the farmers in the valley to begin the journey to take their produce to the harbour. The property has had several owners, including John and Erica Platter who started the *Platter's South African Wine Guide*. It was bought in 2003 by the current owner, who began an extensive redevelopment programme.

Today, this multifaceted property, which includes a winery, two restaurants, a lifestyle boutique, a diamond store and a five-star lodge and spa, was transformed by owner Laurence Graff, the London-born founder and chairman of Graff Diamonds International Ltd, a leading diamond jewellery company with some 36 stores worldwide. The property lies high on the crest of the Helshoogte Pass (which translates as Hell's Heights) and the modern buildings all take maximum advantage of the dramatic views over the valley below all the way to Table Mountain. The opulent interiors were the work of world-renowned architecture and interior design studio David Collins, based in London. The lush, mainly indigenous gardens they are set in were designed and landscaped by celebrity horticulturist Keith Kirsten.

The scale of the operation becomes evident as soon as you enter the oversized double doors and cross the peach-pip and resin floor, the largest in the world, past the glass-walled winery to the restaurant. The personally curated art collection on display has been the lifelong passion of the owner and represents the work of some of South Africa's finest contemporary artists, from Deborah Bell, Sydney Kumalo, Dylan Lewis, Ndikhumbule Ngqinambi, Durant Sihlali and Lionel Smit to Cecil Skotnes. A recent acquisition is Vladimir Tretchikoff's Chinese Girl.

The first wines were made in the new cellar, one of the most advanced and well-equipped facilities in the southern hemisphere, in 2008. Both the

red- and white-wine varieties are equally well represented in the range in terms of number and quality in single-varietal bottlings and blends; there's also a Rosé and a vintage port-style wine. Visitors can sample the range of wines in the sophisticated tasting lounge as well as enjoy a delicious food-and-wine paired tasting.

The interior of the Delaire Graff Restaurant (open daily for lunch and dinner) takes its cue from the charcoal and burnt orange Kentridge that dominates the restaurant, with a striking curved tangerine leather banquette at its centre and an enormous fireplace. The mountain and valley views are breathtaking from the seating on the deck. Under estate executive chef Christiaan Campbell's assured hand, the imaginative cuisine features fresh local produce with many ingredients picked from the estate's own herb and vegetable garden. The Vinoteque, an intimate 18-seater dining and wine-tasting room below the restaurant, caters for private functions. Indochine (open daily for lunch and dinner), is situated at the lodge and spa and offers an Asian-inspired menu. The focal point of this restaurant, with its contemporary beaten copper tables and indigo seating, is the 'Swallows in Flight' installation by artist Lionel Smit.

WWF-SA BIODIVERSITY & WINE INITIATIVE

Established in 2004, the Biodiversity & Wine Initiative (BWI) is a highly successful pioneering partnership between the South African wine industry and conservation sector, now housed within the World Wide Fund for Nature (WWF). To become a BWI member, producers must have at least two hectares of natural or restored natural area on the farm set aside for conservation and should be registered with the Integrated Production of Wine (IPW) scheme and thereby compliant with the industry-prescribed environmental responsibilities. BWI champions are exemplary producers who have an excellent track record as leaders in environmentally responsible farming practices and can be considered as the flagship farms within the industry with regards to the conservation of biodiversity.

To date there are some 27 champions, 17 producer cellar members and 179 members enlisted in the BWI. The total area conserved among them is over 128 000 hectares, which represents close to 130 per cent of the total vineyard footprint in the Cape winelands. You can support participating producers by downloading the BWI winelist or looking for the BWI label on their bottles. **www.wwf.org.za/bwi**

DELHEIM WINES

ADDRESS Knorhoek Road (off the R44), Stellenbosch

GPS S 33° 52′ 10″ E 18° 53′ 08″

TEL +27 (0)21 888 4600

WEBSITE www.delheim.com

TASTING & SALES Daily 09h00 – 17h00 (closed on certain public holidays)

AESTHETIC A dynamic family farm, a favourite among locals and tourists, that has retained its original character while moving with the times

ATTRACTIONS Delheim Restaurant; Oakleaf B&B at DelVera (over the road); gifts and farm produce; cellar tours (daily at 10h30 and 14h30); pre-booked picnics (Sept – Apr)

MUST DO Visit the Collector's Corner at the back of the tasting room for older vintages; throw a coin in the wishing well (proceeds benefit Hospice)

MUST TASTE Vera Cruz Estate Shiraz and the flagship Delheim Grand Reserve; if you enjoy dessert wines try the Edelspatz Noble Late Harvest

Delheim is a much-loved family farm on the slopes of the Simonsberg. Visit the property and there's a good chance you'll meet a member of the friendly Sperling family closely followed by the family dogs. Patriarch Spatz and his wife Vera still live on the farm; daughter Nora and son Victor are directors of the farm. They were recently awarded a KLINK award by Wine Tourism South Africa for a warm family welcome, which acknowledges Delheim as "a family wine farm that offers the warmest country welcome, one that retains the authenticity of its Cape heritage while investing in a cellar-door experience and goes out of its way to make a visit to the cellar door a special experience – making wine tourists feel they are sharing in the special family heritage of the farm and the Cape winelands".

This property on the slopes of the Simonsberg was granted to a German farmer, Lorenz Kamfer, in 1699 and originally named De Drie Sprong. It was acquired by Hans and Del Hoheisen in 1938 with the intention of retiring there. Instead, in 1944 they built a cellar, fitted with storage tanks that were considered revolutionary in design at the time, and started making wine, a labour-intensive task. In the 1950s, when they were no longer able to manage the workload, Del's jovial nephew Michael Sperling set sail from Germany on the *Winchester Castle* to help out on the farm.

Nicknamed 'Spatz', he was to make Delheim a household name, although his first attempts at winemaking were apparently not always appreciated – when a guest declared that the wine tasted bad in no uncertain terms he designed a label of a sparrow pooping into a cask and the infamous 'Spatzendreck' was born! A wine pioneer and one of the industry's great characters, he heralded in a new era at the Cape. Spatz was one of the founders of the Stellenbosch Wine Route in 1971, the first of its kind in South Africa. Four decades later, it's one of the most popular attractions in the Western Cape and there are well-established wine routes in all the regions of the winelands.

The ivy-covered face-brick buildings, shaded by the numerous trees on the property, many of them indigenous, including a 300-year-old yellowwood tree, are well signposted (some amusingly so). Follow the one to the 'Downstairs' cellar and you'll find yourself ensconced in Delheim's tasting room with its famous cobwebbed window. Another atmospheric tasting room is built into the main wine cellar – the 'Vat Cellar', with its hand-carved wine barrels each depicting a chapter from Delheim's history, can accommodate groups of up to 30 people.

The range covers all bases, from the Vera Cruz Estate Shiraz and the Delheim range, to the entry-level Lifestyle label. Added interest comes from

various annual events, from mountain biking to foraging for mushrooms and learning to prepare them, fondue and jazz afternoons, and full-moon hikes at the nearby conservancy. Delheim is a WWF-SA Biodiversity & Wine Initiative Champion.

The Delheim Garden Restaurant (open daily for breakfast and lunch; closed on certain public holidays) lives up to its name – it's set in established gardens with views to Table Mountain in the distance, and you can sit indoors or on one of two patios under shady trees and umbrellas. The relaxed bistro-style eatery offers country fare with traditional German and South African influences, from speciality meats such as bratwurst and Black Forest ham, potato salad, sauerkraut and onion pie, to Weskus snoek fish cakes, Karoo lamb shanks and Cape Malay chicken curry. Jars of the delicious Delheim produce served in the restaurant, including fynbos honey, onion marmalade and pickled pumpkin, can be bought from the tasting room. You can also book a gourmet picnic to enjoy on the riverside lawn next to the cellar. The basket includes a large bottle of sparkling water and you can buy wine to accompany your meal at cellar-door prices. In the event of rain, picnickers are accommodated in the Vat Cellar.

DeMorgenzon

ADDRESS Stellenbosch Kloof Road, Stellenbosch

GPS S 33° 56' 22.99" E18° 45' 0.17"

TEL +27 (0)21 881 3030

WEBSITE www.demorgenzon.co.za

TASTING & SALES Daily 10h00 – 17h00 (closed on certain public holidays)

AESTHETIC The prettiest of properties, floral decadence and whimsical indulgences, an avid gardener's vision brought to life

ATTRACTIONS Tastings on the shady veranda (weather permitting); cellar tours (on request)

MUST DO Stop to smell the roses (and other enchanting blooms) in the gardens and listen to the baroque music being piped to the vineyards 24/7

MUST TASTE The Reserve Chenin Blanc (from a vineyard block planted in 1972)

Wendy and Hylton Appelbaum, both influential businesspeople and philanthropists, bought DeMorgenzon in 2003 and have since totally transformed the 91-hectare property with its 55 hectares of vineyards. At the top of Stellenbosch Kloof and lying across Ribbokkop, the farm rises from about 200 metres to 400 metres above sea level. From this vantage point, panoramic vistas extend from Table Mountain across False Bay to Cape Point and Hangklip, and from the Hottentots Holland mountains to the Helderberg and Simonsberg.

When this dynamic duo refer to DeMorgenzon as 'a garden with vineyards' they're not exaggerating. Watsonias and other wild flowers bloom at the end of vine rows, beds of lavender turn into a broad sweep of purple as you drive up to the tasting room and the gorgeous gardens alone are worth a visit. Trailing wisteria forms a curtain at the edge of a vineyard; flower beds are filled with multi-layered plantings from agapanthus to cannas and roses; there are meadows of wild flowers; and lilies and lotuses fill the interconnected ponds, which were built to direct water from a natural spring. In summer, the surface is covered with exquisite lotus blossoms.

Despite Hylton's penchant for gardening, approximately 10 per cent of the farm was set aside for the restoration of the renosterveld – DeMorgenzon is a member of WWF-SA Biodiversity & Wine Initiative, and the Appelbaums are committed to encouraging biodiversity.

The farm was named DeMorgenzon, which means 'the morning sun', because it is the first part of the Stellenbosch Kloof valley to see the sunrise.

It once formed part of Uiterwyk, one of the oldest farms in the country, which was leased to Dirk Cauchet (also spelt Coetzee and other variations in the records) in 1682 and granted to him by Governor Willem Adriaan van der Stel in 1699. The first road from Cape Town to Stellenbosch ran through this kloof.

Hylton, the founder and chairman of Classic FM, has a passion for music, which is a leitmotif that runs through the property – even the cloakrooms are wallpapered in old music scores! Baroque music is played around the clock to the vines via strategically placed speakers – they firmly believe that the vines respond positively to the power of music when it comes to growth.

If the garden alone is worth a visit to DeMorgenzon then so too are the wines, crafted to express their unique terroir and fruit profile within a classic structure. The compact DMZ core range, strikingly packaged in vivid colours such as Tiffany Blue and Pistachio Green, is complemented by the DeMorgenzon Reserve Chenin Blanc, the Maestro Red and White blends, and Garden Vineyards Rosé. Informative tastings are held in the attractive tasting room or outside on the verandah when the weather permits. The farm's olive oil is also available for purchase from the tasting room.

ERNIE ELS WINES

ADDRESS Annandale Road, Stellenbosch

GPS S 34° 0' 52.8" E 18° 50' 53.5"

TEL +27 (0)21 881 3588

WEBSITE www.ernieelswines.com

TASTING & SALES Mon–Sat 09h00–17h00
(closed on certain public holidays)

AESTHETIC Showpiece winery showcasing
top professional golfer Ernie Els'
passion for wine, as well as his career
achievements, highlights and trophies

ATTRACTIONS Light lunch platters;
tee-box with sweeping vineyard and
mountain views; fun chipping competition
(on the last Fri and Sat of each month);
memorabilia and trophy room; mountain
biking trail; cellar tours

MUST DO Spend some time in the
memorabilia-filled showroom admiring the
impressive collection of trophies on display

MUST TASTE The Portfolio Tasting gives you
a chance to sample all eight wines on offer

"Wine is like golf – in both endeavours nature has the last ruling." Ernie Els, proprietor

The entrance between huge granite boulders via a wooden walkway over koi-filled ponds to world-famous golfer Ernie Els' Helderberg winery is as imposing as his classic golf swing. Inside, big bold masculine spaces with stone walls and *rietdak* ceilings are filled with oversized comfy couches and large-scale wrought-iron light fittings. There's a cavernous fireplace and the focal point is the gleaming copper tasting counter, manned by super-professional staff. From the tasting room's elevated patio are commanding views of the Helderberg Mountain, Stellenbosch and Table Mountain in the distance.

Glass doors lead off the tasting room to the showroom, which has been redesigned and enlarged to house photographs of Ernie in action, family portraits and his impressive collection of trophies.

Through his travels Ernie, one of South Africa's leading sports ambassadors, has tasted some of the world's finest wines. This prompted a decision to produce his eponymous range of wines in 1999. Award-winning winemaker Louis Strydom, who now also heads up the operation as MD, made the maiden 2000 vintage of Ernie Els, a Bordeaux-style blend. This area with its granite-rich soils is renowned for the quality of its red wines and the red-only range features well-structured wines with complexity and depth (be warned, some come with an equally big price tag but all are available for tasting). Large leather-bound menus offer a compact range of lunch choices with a focus on red meat dishes to match the wines. Ernie is also a co-owner of The Big Easy Restaurant at 95 Dorp Street in the town of Stellenbosch.

In the cellar, a spiral staircase takes you down to the private tasting room and Vinoteque, a library that houses the premium wine collection (this can also be accessed via a 'secret passage' formed by the boulders at the entrance). The intimate space can be booked for a tasting of rare wine offerings paired with fine food (accommodates a maximum of eight people).

FLAGSTONE WINERY

"Every bottle of Flagstone wine is a journey with many twists and turns. It can never be hurried and there are no short cuts." Bruce Jack, winemaker

Flagstone may be a relatively small winery but its output is prolific and it has notched up its fair share of awards for these handcrafted, distinctive wines. There are several ranges and each wine has a story behind it. Evocative names in the extensive core Flagstone range include cult red blend Dragon Tree, Dark Horse Shiraz, Music Room Cabernet Sauvignon, Word of Mouth Viognier, Writer's Block Pinotage and the Treaty Tree Reserve White.

Also available for tasting are the Kumala wines, which share the same owner as Flagstone, Accolade Wines South Africa. Constellation Wines South Africa acquired the Kumala brand in 2006 and Flagstone in 2008 before the new entity, Accolade Wines South Africa, was formed in January 2011.

Equipped with a political science and English degree from the University of Cape Town, winemaker and founder Bruce Jack completed his masters in literature at St Andrews University in Scotland in 1991. He then became the first South African to study winemaking at Roseworthy in Australia before working several overseas vintages to gain hands-on experience.

Bruce returned to South Africa and started his own venture in 1999. From the outset he approached things differently. His first winery was at the V&A Waterfront in Cape Town and key to its operation was a massive chilling unit. Grapes were brought in from various growers, some of whom he now has joint ventures with. Grapes are sourced from five core vineyards and Flagstone is very involved in the management of their growers' vineyards. These stretch from the southernmost winegrowing area, Elim, to one of the most easterly vineyards high in the Swartberg and inland to the Breede valley. Flagstone is committed to the wine industry's world-leading Integrated Production of Wine (IPW) scheme and is a member of the WWF-SA Biodiversity & Wine Initiative.

Since 2002, the winery has been housed in what was originally a dynamite factory, erected in 1901 and part of Cecil John Rhodes' empire. It was flagged for demolition when Flagstone moved into the industrial space and converted it into a winery. The tasting facility was moved to Stellenbosch for a few years but since moving back here mid-2012 they've experienced more feet through the door than ever before.

ADDRESS AECI, Heartland Properties, De Beers Avenue, Somerset West

GPS S 34° 5' 26.38" E 18° 48' 30.04"

TEL +27 (0)21 852 5052

WEBSITE www.flagstonewines.com

TASTING & SALES Mon–Fri 10h00–16h00; Sat 10h00–15h00

AESTHETIC Double-volume industrial space behind steel doors with a corner allocated to wine tasting

ATTRACTIONS Cellar tours (by appointment); Cheetah Outreach and Triggerfish Brewery are housed on the same property

MUST DO Find out what's behind the name of each wine

MUST TASTE Many excellent wines to choose from so follow your personal preferences. For Pinotage fans, try the elegant Writer's Block Pinotage and Dragon Tree, a Cape blend

HIDDEN VALLEY

ADDRESS Annandale Road, Stellenbosch

GPS S 34° 1' 14.2" E 18° 51' 12.9"

TEL +27 (0)21 880 2646

WEBSITE www.hiddenvalleywines.com

TASTING & SALES Daily 09h00 – 17h00

AESTHETIC Modern clean-lined winery with
an impressive stone wall surrounded by
almond orchards, olive groves and vineyards

ATTRACTIONS Overture Restaurant; cheese
or chocolate platters; pre-booked picnics;
Friday evening sundowners – a glass
of wine and a cheese platter (weather
permitting, booking advised); table olives,
olive oil and tapenade; walks/hikes; cellar
tours (by appointment)

MUST DO Taste the peppery olive oil – the
table olives and tapenade are delicious
too; book a picnic (at least three days in
advance) to enjoy beside the dam in the
beautiful indigenous garden

MUST TASTE The Pinotage stands out but
as it's a small, terroir-specific range it's
worth tasting all the wines

"We only have brief custody of this land and when I hand it on to whoever and whenever, I want to ensure that the farm is more eco-valuable than when I purchased it."

Dave Hidden, owner

This secluded farm, set on a mountain slope affording 180-degree views from Cape Town to the Simonsberg, was the reward for years of determination and patience by Dave Hidden, a trained winemaker and entrepreneur. It was pointed out to him by his viticulture professor at Stellenbosch University, the late Chris Orffer, who rated it "the best vineyard soil in South Africa". Dave heeded this advice and finally acquired this parcel of land high on the Helderberg slopes in 1998. A Gauteng-based industrialist at the time, he took up residence on the farm in 2006.

The contemporary gravity-fed cellar blends into the environment. Its impressive stone wall was built by Sardinian-born stonemason, Luigi Tucconi, whose uncle taught him the skill. The winery overlooks a dam with indigenous gardens and is surrounded by vineyards, almond orchards and silvery olive groves. A total of 4 000 olive trees, both oil and table varieties, were planted and products include high-quality extra virgin olive oil, table olives and tapenade. Walking paths have been laid out for visitors to enjoy the natural spaces with their abundant birdlife.

Sustainability is the philosophy that drives the farm, a member of the WWF-SA Biodiversity & Wine Initiative. This approach, demonstrated by their ethos of 'working with nature', is incorporated into all its daily activities; recycling has become a mantra and Hidden Valley is farmed according to ecologically sensitive farming practices, from preparing the soils and managing the vines to conserving non-agricultural land.

The vineyards lie high up on the Helderberg slopes and benefit from the cooling breezes that blow in from False Bay, which is some five kilometres away. The terroir-specific wines are made in a non-interventionist way at this quality-driven boutique winery. The once compact range comprising two red blends, Hidden Gems and Hidden Secrets, a Pinotage and a Sauvignon Blanc has been expanded to include a food-friendly Chenin Blanc, and a Méthode Cap Classique Brut and Rosé.

Wine tasting takes place inside the tasting centre or on the terrace outside where you can fully appreciate the views. The specially designed chocolate

and wine pairing, the Chocolatier's Platter, is a very popular option. You can also taste the table olives, tapenade and deliciously peppery olive oil, which you can buy in a convenient, cleverly packaged two-litre 'integrity pack' that seals the oil from light and oxygen. Gourmet picnic baskets, which include a bottle of wine, are also available (book at least three days in advance).

Award-winning chef Bertus Basson, whose food ethos is 'local and fresh every day', opened Overture (open for lunch Wednesday to Sunday; dinner Thursday to Saturday) at the end of 2007. The menu changes regularly according to what ingredients are available. The winelist features Hidden Valley wines, including a Viognier exclusive to the restaurant, as well as a small, well-chosen selection of wines from other producers. Be sure to phone well in advance to secure a booking.

JORDAN WINE ESTATE

"A little bit of my heart and soul goes into every barrel and every bottle. The watchword is quality, not quantity."

Gary Jordan, owner

This family-owned farm at the top of the secluded and scenic Stellenbosch Kloof boasts spectacular panoramic views of Table Mountain, False Bay and Stellenbosch from its hillside vineyards. Ted and Sheelagh Jordan bought the property in 1982 and implemented an extensive replanting programme, matching classic varieties and various clones to the most suitable soils and slopes. Son Gary, a geologist, and his wife Kathy, an economist, have been making wines on the farm since 1993. They honed their craft by gaining practical experience in California and returned to South Africa to build a cellar on the farm in 1992. The gravity-flow cellar is recessed into the mountain slope for natural cooling. Fruit from individual vineyards is vinified separately in stainless steel tanks. The barrel-fermented whites are made according to traditional Burgundian methods, and separate barrel cellars have been designated for Cabernet Sauvignon, Merlot and Shiraz to undergo malolactic fermentation.

From the first vintage, this dynamic husband-and-wife team has produced compelling and individual wines. The comprehensive Jordan Estate range is the top tier and includes the much-acclaimed single-vineyard Nine Yards Chardonnay (for which they went 'the whole nine yards') and Cobblers Hill, a barrel-selected Bordeaux-style red blend.

The Jordan family, who have always protected the gentle Cape dwarf chameleon, a natural pest-controller, were concerned that they might be harmed by the machine harvesters in the vineyards. They started the Jordan Chameleon Research Bursary whereby proceeds from worldwide sales are awarded annually to a PhD student in the specific study of chameleon research in the Cape winelands. This is how the Chameleon range, which comprises a white and a red blend, a Rosé and a no-added-sulphur Merlot, got its name. Research fortunately discovered that in general they are not found in the vineyards, preferring bushes and shrubs. The indigenous bushes and reeds around the winery and restaurant are home to numerous chameleons, which have become a visitor attraction at the farm. This easy-drinking range complements the premium Jordan Estate range and well-priced Bradgate range. The wines from all three ranges are available for sampling at the tasting room (unless a particular vintage is sold out).

ADDRESS Stellenbosch Kloof Road, Stellenbosch

GPS S 33° 56' 33.7" E 18° 44' 41.3"

TEL +27 (0)21 881 3441

WEBSITE www.jordanwines.com

TASTING & SALES Daily 09h30–16h30 (closed on certain public holidays)

AESTHETIC Family farm with lush lawns, friendly dogs, a dam bordered by weavers' nests and teeming with water birds

ATTRACTIONS Jordan Restaurant and Deli; walks/hikes; mountain biking; fly fishing – catch and release (booking essential); visits to old prospectors' mine shafts; cellar tours (by appointment); B&B guest accommodation (from mid-2014)

MUST DO Book a vintage tasting; soak in one of the loveliest views of the Stellenbosch mountain bowl; spot shy Cape dwarf chameleons clinging to the reeds in front of the restaurant

MUST TASTE Nine Yards Chardonnay (when not out of stock) and Cobblers Hill, a red blend, both flagship wines

WINE TIP The Chameleon Merlot No Added Sulphur is a good buy for those who are sensitive to sulphur

If you've had a tough week at work or are just celebrating the start of a weekend in the winelands, you can make a booking for the monthly Wine-down Friday, which pairs wine and canapés; you can also book an exclusive tour of the vineyards as sunset approaches.

Jordan Restaurant (open for lunch Tuesday to Sunday, and Monday in season; dinner Thursday and Friday, and Saturday in season), a contemporary bistro, is among the top eateries in the winelands. There's an open-plan kitchen that allows you to see the chefs at work and a deck with views over the dam, vineyards and the Stellenbosch mountains in the distance. At the helm is skilled chef George Jardine, who uses locally sourced ingredients, some of them from the restaurant's own kitchen garden. The restaurant is also equipped with a barrel smoker and a wood-fired oven. His wife Louise manages the front of house. Menus change daily, but the format for lunch (a two- or three-course option) and dinner (the dégustation menu of six courses with matching wines) remains the same throughout the year. Dishes change according to seasonal availability; signatures include starters such as the aromatic Asian-flavoured Saldanha Bay mussels en papillote, and for mains the aged Chalmar beef fillet. The Cheese Room, which you can visit for your dessert course if you choose, stocks South African cheese, most of it made by artisanal producers. The backbone of the wine list is Jordan wines but there are some excellent other choices.

Jordan now boasts a deli, also run by George, offering a selection of breads, pastries, charcuterie and a dish of the day that visitors can enjoy in the deli, on the veranda of the tasting room or on the lawns at the dam.

GREEN WINERIES

The South African wine industry is a world leader in production integrity. Along with the producers' commitment to farming sustainably there has been a growth in the number of wineries that are converting to organic and/or biodynamic winegrowing practices. Others are going off the grid and reducing their carbon footprint. Some of these 'green' wineries feature elsewhere in this book; others within an easy hour's drive from Cape Town that are worth a visit include Avondale, in Paarl, which combines organic and biodynamic principles (tastings by appointment only – you can also book an Eco Tour of the farm). Also in Paarl, Backsberg Estate Cellars has the distinction of being the first South African farm to attain carbon neutral status, and Joostenberg's wines were certified organic from the 2012 vintage. In Stellenbosch, Laibach Vineyards, which has been producing wines naturally for over a decade, is well known for its organic Ladybird range, and Reyneke Wines, which has 'Quality with integrity' as its mantra, has won numerous awards for its biodynamic wines. Wedderwill Wine Estate (by appointment only), is a biodynamic farm on the foothills of the Hottentots Holland Mountain just outside of Somerset West.

www.avondalewine.co.za | www.backsberg.co.za
www.joostenberg.com | www.laibachwines.com
www.reynekewines.co.za | www.wedderwill.co.za

KANONKOP ESTATE

Johann and Paul Krige are the fourth-generation custodians of this family estate on the slopes of the Simonsberg mountains. Its name, Kanonkop, was derived from the nearby koppie from which a cannon was fired in the Seventeenth century to alert the farmers in outlying areas that ships voyaging between Europe and the Far East had entered Table Bay. The farmers would then load their wagons, inspan their oxen and set off for Cape Town to barter their produce – mainly fresh fruit and vegetables – with the sailors and travellers who had spent many long months at sea.

Today, the focus remains firmly on producing quality red wines. Pinotage comes in various guises, from the top-tier limited-release Kanonkop Black Label Pinotage, made from bush vines that are now over 60 years old (available for purchase but not for tasting); to the Kanonkop Pinotage; and in a Cape blend, Kadette, and the Kadette Pinotage Dry Rosé. A Cabernet Sauvignon and Paul Sauer, a seamless traditional Bordeaux-style blend, complete the compact range.

Kanonkop's legendary snoek braais, served with traditional accompaniments from *soetpatat* to *korrelkonfyt* and *potbrood*, have gained an international reputation over the past two decades. They are offered all year round by appointment only (minimum 15 people). In the summer months, you can enjoy a cheese platter paired with a glass of red wine under shady oak trees.

ADDRESS R44, Stellenbosch

GPS S 33° 51′ 18.4″ E 18° 51′ 36.1″

TEL +27 (0)21 884 4656

WEBSITE www.kanonkop.co.za

TASTING & SALES Mon – Fri 09h00 – 17h00; Sat 09h00 – 14h00; public holidays 10h00 – 16h00 (closed on certain ones)

AESTHETIC A family-owned and -run estate on the foothills of the Simonsberg with an enviable track record for consistent excellence over decades

ATTRACTIONS Art gallery; enjoy cheese platters under the oak trees in summer; traditional snoek barbecues (by appointment only, minimum 15 people); cellar tours; private tasting room (pre-booked only)

MUST DO Read the handwritten anecdotes and highlights of each year, represented by a wall covered in bottles from each vintage

MUST TASTE The range is compact so it's worth tasting all the wines, but note the Kanonkop Black Label Pinotage is available only for purchase, not tasting

KLEINE ZALZE WINES

The winemaking tradition at Kleine Zalze dates back to 1695, and through the years wine has been made on the farm by many of the various well-known families who have owned it. In 1996, Kobus Basson, who had at the time been in legal practice for 15 years in Stellenbosch, and his family purchased the property. Since then, the cellar has been extensively renovated and modernised, and a maturation cellar excavated beneath it, while retaining its sense of history. The vineyards were also replanted with new clones. Rolf Schulz, Kobus' business partner, bought his brother-in-law Jan Malan's share in 2005.

Also part of the property is the De Zalze Winelands Estate, a luxury residential development, and De Zalze Golf Course, one of only three golf clubs in the world set on a working wine farm (another also in South Africa is Steenberg Vineyards on page 22). The 18-hole golf course, by world-renowned golf course designer, Peter Matkovich, opened in 2002. Set alongside the first fairway of the golf course is the Kleine Zalze Lodge, a boutique hotel that opened in 2005.

Kleine Zalze is planted to premium varieties on south-facing slopes with well-drained dark red soils, allowing for even ripening of fruit. In 2002, Kleine Zalze acquired the vineyards on the neighbouring farm, Groote Zalze, as well. These are planted to Sauvignon Blanc, and red-wine varieties Cabernet Franc, Cabernet Sauvignon, Merlot and Shiraz. Grapes are also sourced from specially selected vineyards that include blocks with old bush vine plantings and some in cooler coastal-climate areas.

Kleine Zalze offers four clearly defined ranges – the Foot of Africa range, the Cellar Selection range, the Vineyard Selection range and the flagship Family Reserve range – all of which offer good value. Informative tastings are conducted at the tasting room counter or under the oaks at tables on the terrace just outside.

Completing the winelands lifestyle experience is the award-winning Terroir restaurant (open daily for lunch, and dinner Monday to Saturday), which was opened in 2004 by chef-patron Michael Broughton, who creates fresh, flavoursome dishes. The chalkboard menu changes according to what's in season and features daily specials. The rustic Tuscan-style eatery with its tabled terrace overlooks a pond and lovely gardens, with beautiful mountain views up the valley.

Meerlust Estate

Owner Hannes Myburgh is the eighth-generation custodian of Meerlust. This historic Seventeenth-century estate at the end of a palm and oak lined driveway has been owned by the family since 1756. Hannes completed a Bachelor of Arts degree majoring in French and English at Stellenbosch University before studying winemaking at Geisenheim in Germany.

The first owner of the property was a German immigrant named Henning Huising who settled here in 1693 and named his farm Meerlust, meaning 'love of the sea', as it is near False Bay.

In 1960, Hannes' parents Nico and Jean Myburgh began a 'renaissance' of the farm, with its manor house, wine cellar, family cemetery and beautiful, rare dovecote. New vineyards were planted and extensive restoration of the Cape Dutch buildings started out with the manor house. Meerlust was declared a national monument in 1987.

Under the guidance of Hannes and current winemaker Chris Williams, this rejuvenation has continued, with the buying back of original farmland, resiting of vineyards according to soil surveys and satellite mapping, and an ongoing vine renewal programme. The cellar was modernised, and picking times for optimal ripeness and label design were tweaked.

Meerlust is situated some 15 kilometres from Stellenbosch and five kilometres from False Bay. Evening mists roll in from the nearby ocean to cool the vineyards, allowing the grapes to ripen slowly, and achieve concentrated and complex flavours. The red-focused range consists of a Cabernet

ADDRESS Baden Powell Drive (R310), Stellenbosch

GPS S 34° 1' 1.7" E 18° 45' 24.7"

TEL +27 (0)21 843 3587

WEBSITE www.meerlust.co.za

TASTING & SALES Mon – Fri 09h00 – 17h00; Sat 10h00 – 14h00 (closed public holidays)

AESTHETIC Aristocratic Cape estate with enduring appeal

ATTRACTIONS Historic manor house, cellar and dovecote; bird sanctuary; cellar tours (by appointment)

MUST DO Take a look at the fascinating photographic timeline and soak up the sense of history that permeates the estate

MUST TASTE Rubicon, a South African classic

Sauvignon, Merlot, Pinot Noir and a Bordeaux-style blend, Rubicon, as well as a barrel-fermented Chardonnay, the first being vintage 1995. The flagship red, Rubicon, which had its maiden vintage in 1980, has since established itself as a South African icon. It was the result of a collaboration between then owner and winemaker team Nico Myburgh and Giorgio Dalla Cia, and was among the earliest of the Cape Bordeaux-style reds (the Welgemeend Estate Reserve preceded it by a year).

The bottling of the wines is handled on site by Companjiesdrift Bottling & Logistics, a joint venture between the Meerlust Workers Trust and the Myburgh Family Trust. Social and environmental sustainability are top priorities.

The wine shop boasts a fascinating photographic timeline, which reflects the history both of the estate and of the Cape. Private tastings are available (by appointment only) and groups larger than 10 are also required to make a reservation. The eclectic interior of the tasting facility offers a cool respite from summer heat, while in the winter a crackling fire welcomes visitors. Laid-back music creates the perfect ambience for tasting wine.

MULDERBOSCH VINEYARDS

ADDRESS M12, Stellenbosch

GPS S 33° 53' 22.8" E 18° 49' 8.3"

TEL +27 (0)21 881 8140

WEBSITE www.mulderbosch.co.za

TASTING & SALES Tues–Sun 10h00–18h00
(closed on certain public holidays)

AESTHETIC Modern, simple but stylish with
a great indoor-outdoor flow

ATTRACTIONS Gourmet pizzas, and cheese
and charcuterie platters; two professional
bocce courts

MUST DO Play a game of bocce (Italian
boules); enjoy a delicious thin-based wood-
fired gourmet pizza, each topping designed
to partner a specific wine in the range

MUST TASTE The focus is on Chenin Blanc –
a vertical flight of older vintages makes for
an interesting tasting experience

Former intensive care doctor Larry Jacobs bought Mulderbosch in 1989. Winemaker Mike Dobrovic joined him and together they cleaned up the farm, planted the first vineyards and built a cellar. Mulderbosch rapidly gained an international reputation for the quality of its wine, initially the Sauvignon Blanc, and recognition for its distinctive labels, designed by Mike, who has a philosophical bent and found inspiration in a Cuban cigar band!

In 2010, Mulderbosch was bought by California-based investment company Terroir Capital, which boasts some impressive wine assets, including Sandhi and Leviathan in California, Maison L'Oree in Burgundy and Fable in South Africa. Charles Banks, who has a long-held love of South Africa, is a founding and managing partner of Terroir Capital, as well as the senior executive editor of Fine Wine Magazines, which has built a global readership of over two million. Charles was also formerly a co-owner and managing partner of Californian cult winery, Screaming Eagle. The Mulderbosch brand moved from its original location off the R304 to a larger, modern winery off the Polkadraai Road in the Stellenbosch Hills (on what used to be its sister property Kanu, with which it swapped places).

Taking Mulderbosch to the next level has seen significant improvements in both the vineyards and the cellar, with investment in new cooling equipment for the white wines and smaller tanks for red-wine production. The farm has 45 hectares planted to various varieties and they also buy in grapes from 11 regions, where each carefully chosen vineyard is micro-managed by grower-partners. Mulderbosch, a member of WWF-SA Biodiversity & Wine Initiative, follows environmentally responsible management practices both in the cellar and vineyards and on the land.

Mulderbosch has a rich lineage of old-vine Chenin Blancs and Charles, who has a special interest in Chenin Blanc, plans to invest further in the variety and add site-specific single-vineyard Chenins to the wine portfolio. This includes Faithful Hound, a red blend, a selection of Chardonnays and Chenin Blancs, a Sauvignon Blanc and Sauvignon NLH, and a Cabernet Sauvignon Rosé. There are still some vintages made by Mike on offer in the tasting room, along with those made by current winemaker Adam Mason, who was previously the winemaker at Klein Constantia (see page 18). Terroir Capital's consultant winemaker Andy Erickson, who lives and works in the Napa Valley where he made wine at Screaming Eagle among others, consults to both Mulderbosch and sister property Fable Wines in Tulbagh.

Visitors to Mulderbosch can also taste Adam's own duo of Yardstick wines (a Chardonnay and a Pinot Noir) and a trio of excellent wines from

Fable: Bobbejaan, a Shiraz; and Lion's Whisker and Jackal's Bird, a red and a white blend respectively. Mulderbosch also sells specially selected artisanal beers from Brewers & Union and Coopers Brewery (available for tasting only over the weekends), and Italian coffee.

   The relaxed, family-friendly tasting room has been transformed and extended into an outdoor space, with wooden decking lined with comfy cushioned seating, beanbags for the lawn, and landscaped areas where you can relax and eat while taking advantage of the views of vineyards and rolling hills. Bold usage of red in the tasting room reflects Mulderbosch's signature crimson seal. There's comfortable seating on chairs and couches, and a big fireplace with roaring fires in winter. The thin-based rustic pizzas (available from 12h00 to 16h00), which are cooked in an outdoor wood-burning pizza oven, have a variety of delicious fresh toppings designed to complement the wines in the Mulderbosch range.

MURATIE WINE ESTATE

ADDRESS Knorhoek Road (off the R44), Stellenbosch

GPS S 33° 52′ 14.8″ E 18° 52′ 35.1″

TEL +27 (0)21 865 2330/36

WEBSITE www.muratie.co.za

TASTING & SALES Daily 10h00–17h00 (closed Good Friday, 25 Dec & 1 Jan)

AESTHETIC One of the most atmospheric wine estates in the Cape with a rich history; every wine tells a story

ATTRACTIONS Farm Kitchen (light lunches and cheese platters); summer music concerts; art gallery; The Canitz Studio guest cottage; cellar tours (by appointment)

MUST DO Try a port and chocolate pairing

MUST TASTE The flagship red blend, Ansela van de Caab – but make sure you hear the fascinating story of the slave woman behind the name of the wine first; also the Pinot Noir, as they are one of only a few Stellenbosch producers of this fickle grape

"In the autumn I have an irresistable urge towards Muratie – the melancholy, the sweet passing of the season, resides in the farm's name." Hennie Aucamp, author

Tucked away near the top of the lovely Knorhoek valley in the foothills of the Simonsberg – you literally drive through Muratie to get to Delheim (see page 112) – this unique estate has a rich history that's still in evidence in every nook and cranny of the property, with its ancient oaks and atmospheric tasting room and cellar. Muratie's name stems from the Dutch word *murasie*, which means ruins. Today owned by Rijk Melck and his family, the farm dates back to 1685, making it one of the oldest estates in the country.

The wines are as characterful as the atmospheric farm itself and the back labels are worth a read too. Steeped in history, most of Muratie's wines are named after characters from its colourful past. There's the flagship Ansela van de Caab (a red blend) and Laurens Campher (a white blend), and the Ronnie Melck Shiraz Family Selection. In the premium range there's the Isabella Chardonnay, Alberta Annemarie Merlot, George Paul Canitz Pinot Noir (this variety was planted on the farm in 1927, the first in South Africa), Ronnie Melck Shiraz and the Lady Alice Méthode Cap Classique. There's also Ben Prins, a port-style wine, and Amber Forever, a fortified dessert wine named after one of Canitz' models (you can view the painting of her in the cellar), as well as a Cape Ruby and a Late Bottled Vintage. The Melck's range of Sauvignon Blanc, Cabernet Franc Rosé and Shiraz-Cabernet completes the line-up.

While the tasting room, filled with untouched cobwebs and with an 80-year-old family table as its centrepiece, caters for walk-in visitors, you can also book a personal tasting in advance. Make sure that you make time to find out the fascinating stories behind the labels. Home-made treats such as jam, rusks and Muratie's famous nougat are also for sale in the tasting room.

Rijk's wife Kim oversees the preparation of the honest farm fare served at Muratie's Farm Kitchen (open daily for lunch), such as soup with freshly baked farm bread, chicken salad or curry and rice. Lamb shanks and oxtail are on offer in the wintertime. In summer, you can have lunch in the courtyard under the old oak trees; in winter you can enjoy your meal in the cosy atmosphere of the old fermentation tanks in the cellar with its fireplace for warmth, surrounded by GP Canitz's paintings. Bird-watching enthusiasts can track the latest sitings at Muratie on their website. There is also a live music programme in summer.

RUST EN VREDE ESTATE

ADDRESS Annandale Road, Stellenbosch

GPS S 33° 59' 54.0" E 18° 51' 22.5"

TEL +27 (0)21 881 3881

WEBSITE www.rustenvrede.com

TASTING & SALES Mon–Sat 09h00–17h00
(closed on certain public holidays)

AESTHETIC An impressive Cape estate, rich
in heritage; well-maintained historic Cape
Dutch buildings surrounded by ancient
oak trees and gracious gardens combine
seamlessly with a modern sensibility

ATTRACTIONS Rust en Vrede Restaurant
(open for dinner only); cellar tours; gift shop

MUST DO Take time to admire the lovely
mountain vistas and immaculate gardens,
the foundation for which was laid by
current proprietor Jean Engelbrecht's
mother, Ellen

MUST TASTE Limited Edition – a tasting of
the Estate blend and 1694 Classification
(some of the wines in the red-only range
are pricey but even the most expensive is
available for tasting)

"The challenge of owning Rust en Vrede is not just to maintain it – that is your responsibility – but to build on it."

Jean Engelbrecht, owner

Rust en Vrede (which means rest and peace) was established in 1694 by Governor of the Cape, Willem Adriaan van der Stel. It was originally made up of a larger property but in the early 1700s this was divided into two, with one section remaining as Rust en Vrede. In 1780, the first house was built on the estate, followed by the cellar in 1785 and a larger manor house in 1790. Its front gable was destroyed in a fire in 1823 hence the date on the front gable is 1825, the year it was rebuilt. All three buildings are National Monuments.

The farm, which had become neglected, was bought in 1977 by legendary Springbok rugby player Jannie Engelbrecht, who set about restoring it to its former grandeur and establishing it as a premium red-wine estate. Rust en Vrede's current proprietor, former pilot Jean Engelbrecht, grew up on the farm and it's where he still lives today. The iconic estate has been under his aegis since 1998.

Over the years, many accolades and awards have been bestowed on the estate. One of the most memorable was when a Rust en Vrede wine was chosen by President Nelson Mandela to be served at the 1994 Nobel Peace Prize dinner in Oslo. Another highlight was when the family hosted an official lunch for the Queen of Denmark at their manor house.

Rust en Vrede's temperature-controlled underground cellar, the first of its kind for a privately owned South African winery, was designed by renowned architect Gawie Fagan. Rust en Vrede was also the first winery in the country to specialise exclusively in the production of red wine. Situated on the low-lying slopes of the Helderberg and sheltered from the prevailing winds, the estate enjoys a warmer mesoclimate, which prompted this decision.

Rust en Vrede has built a reputation for top quality. The range of full-bodied red wines encompasses three varietal wines – a Cabernet Sauvignon, Merlot and Shiraz – and the Single Vineyard Syrah, as well as two blends: one of South Africa's most expensive red wines, the 1694 Classification, and the Estate. The tasting room is manned by friendly, well-informed staff. You can also enjoy a tasting outdoors on the patio on sunny days.

The original old barrel cellar, a National Monument, was converted into

a contemporary restaurant while still retaining its character. Rust en Vrede Restaurant opened its doors at the end of 2007 (dinner only, Tuesday to Saturday, booking advised). Comfortable chairs, soft lighting and the finest tableware, from crockery by potter David Walters, to Riedel stemware and Laguiole knives, coupled with faultless service make for one of the top fine dining experiences in the winelands. Executive chef John Shuttleworth and his team prepare dishes based on classical French cuisine with modern nuances. There is a four-course and a six-course menu. The restaurant has its own vegetable and herb garden. A substantial and superb wine list includes Rust en Vrede back vintages, wines from the Cape Winemakers Guild, and a selection of French Champagne.

Although the restaurant is only open for dinner, a one-course winemaker's lunch of steak, French fries, a garden salad and a glass of wine is available at the tasting room (Tuesday to Saturday).

RUSTENBERG WINES

ADDRESS Rustenberg Road, Stellenbosch

GPS S 33° 53′ 44.8″ E 18° 53′ 33.6″

Tel +27 (0)21 809 1200

WEBSITE www.rustenberg.co.za

TASTING & SALES Mon – Fri 09h00 – 16h30;
Sat 10h00 – 16h00; Sun 10h00 – 15h00
(closed on certain public holidays)

AESTHETIC A prestigious property that
graciously reflects a bygone era

ATTRACTIONS Picture-perfect gardens

MUST DO Wander through the beautiful
gardens and while away the time on a
bench surrounded by flowers, trees, birds
and insects

MUST TASTE Try the flagship red blend
John X Merriman, a Cape benchmark;
the wines in the Site Specific range: Peter
Barlow, a 100% Cabernet Sauvignon; Five
Soldiers Chardonnay; and the Syrahs

Driving into Ida's Valley and up the winding driveway to Rustenberg takes you past cattle grazing in green pastures to this Cape gem, which was founded in 1682. Rustenberg, with its historic gabled manor house, gardens, vineyards and the Simonsberg mountain standing sentinel over it, is breathtakingly beautiful.

Its winegrowing history dates back to first owner Roelof Pasman from Meurs near the Rhine, who recognised its winegrowing potential. By 1781, some 3 000 cases of wine were produced on the farm. By the end of the century, production was doubled by his son Pieter, who inherited the farm, and a new cellar was built. Wine has been bottled at this cellar continuously since 1892.

In the early 1800s, then owner Jacob Eksteen divided Rustenberg into two and a section was given to his son-in-law, who named it Schoongezicht and sold it soon thereafter. Rustenberg and Schoongezicht were at their peak around 1812, with magnificent homesteads and flourishing vineyards, but these were devastated by the disease phylloxera, which was coupled with a recession. In 1892 John X Merriman (who later became Prime Minister of the Cape), bought Schoongezicht and his brother-in-law, Sir Jacob Barry, bought Rustenberg two years later.

In 1941, Peter and Pamela Barlow bought Rustenberg. They later acquired Schoongezicht and the two properties became one farm again. Peter lovingly restored many of the old buildings on the farm, developed the farming capacity by building dams and renovated the winery. Their son Simon took over the running of the farm in 1987 and revitalised the property by building a new winery and replanting the vineyards. Son Murray, having completed his Masters in Oenology at the University of Adelaide in Australia, is primarily involved on the winemaking and marketing side. The Barlows have been at Rustenberg for over 70 years, which is the longest period any one family has owned the farm.

In 2001, Simon's wife, Rozanne, regenerated and restored the gardens situated next to the Cape Dutch homestead, Schoongezicht. The old tennis court was transformed into a labyrinth, which follows the design of the one at Chartres Cathedral in France, and the 25-metre swimming pool was converted into a lily pond filled with colourful Koi fish. The pergola, originally built by John X Merriman, supports fragrant climbers such as roses and clematis. The distinct quadrants in this formal English garden are accessed by brick pathways.

The vineyards that produce grapes for the Rustenberg wines climb the

rich red slopes of the Simonsberg. All grapes are hand-harvested in the early mornings, often over a fortnight to optimise quality and ripeness, and all vineyard blocks are vinified separately, and then blended for added complexity, with ratios depending on each specific vintage.

The consistently strong portfolio focuses on classic varieties. The Site Specific range includes the flagship Peter Barlow Cabernet Sauvignon (imbibed by James Bond in *Carte Blanche* by Jeffrey Deaver); and the Five Soldiers Chardonnay. Then there's the Regional range, spearheaded by the flagship John X Merriman, and encompassing RM Nicholson (a red blend named after Rustenberg's first winemaker), a wooded and an unwooded Chardonnay, a Sauvignon Blanc, a Merlot, two Syrahs and the Straw Wine. There's a Roussanne in this range too – Rustenberg pioneered the growing of this variety in South Africa and made the first single varietal wine out it. It's still one of only a handful in the country, so make a note to taste it too.

Housed in what was once the farm's horse stables, the tasting room is understated and contemporary. The interior was redesigned in 1999 by Stellenbosch architect Simon Beerstecher, who is now based in the UK. A spiral staircase takes you from the upper level of the centre to the tasting area with its curved counter made of old wine barrels.

SIMONSIG ESTATE

ADDRESS Kromme Rhee Road (M23, between the R304 and R44), Stellenbosch

GPS S 33° 52′ 14.19″ E 18° 49′ 34.92″

TEL +27 (0)21 888 4900

WEBSITE www.simonsig.co.za

TASTING & SALES Mon – Fri 08h30 – 17h00; Sat 08h30 – 16h00; Sun 11h00 – 15h00 (closed on certain public holidays)

AESTHETIC Established family wine estate, a landmark with a reputation for innovation and genuine hospitality

ATTRACTIONS Cuvée restaurant; 4x4 Land Rover Experience; labyrinth vineyard; exhibition vineyard showcasing various varieties; cellar tours (weekdays at 10h00 & 15h00, Sat 10h00, booking advised)

MUST DO The Kaapse Vonkel cellar tour (bookings only, for groups of 10 or more) followed by a tasting and sabrage – this ceremonial opening of bubbly using a sabre always draws a crowd

MUST TASTE The bubbles – the first Méthode Cap Classique in the country was produced here, after all

This leading wine estate, named after its striking views of the Simonsberg mountain, was one of the founding members of the Stellenbosch Wine Route. It is owned by the Malan family, whose forebear, French Huguenot Jacques Malan, set foot in the Cape in 1688 and was given land on which to plant new vineyards.

In 1953 his descendant Frans Malan started wine farming on his father-in-law's farm, De Hoop. In 1964 he bought his second property and named it Simonsig, which formed the nucleus of the Simonsig wine estate of today. He replanted the vineyards during the early 1960s, and bottled and sold his first wines under the Simonsig label in 1968. Two years later, the first reds were released. From these humble beginnings, Simonsig has grown into a family business with a solid reputation. Since 1978 Frans' three sons, Pieter, Francois and Johan, have continued the tradition and formed a partnership to manage Simonsig.

The pioneering patriarch of the family made a significant contribution to the South African wine industry. He was instrumental in starting the Stellenbosch Wine Route in 1971 and in that same year he also produced South Africa's very first sparkling wine made according to the traditional Méthode Champenoise (in the Cape this later became known as Méthode Cap Classique). The maiden vintage was made from Chenin Blanc and he named it Kaapse Vonkel (Cape Sparkle). During the 1970s, he also produced the first Rhine Riesling and wooded white wines in the country. In 1987, his son Johan, the cellarmaster, changed the Kaapse Vonkel 'recipe' to Chardonnay, Pinot Noir and Pinot Meunier, and Kaapse Vonkel became the first Méthode Cap Classique in the country to contain all three of the classic varieties used in Champagne.

The vineyards cover 210 hectares of mountain foothills. Unique to Simonsig is the world's first productive vineyard planted in the shape of a labyrinth; it consists of 350 Cabernet Sauvignon vines, which were planted in 2003. Next to it near the entranceway is a small vineyard showcasing a wide number of different varieties.

Simonsig has a number of wines on offer for tasting, many of them award-winning benchmarks. While Méthode Cap Classique is an obvious place to start, if the line-up leaves you feeling swamped here are a few more suggestions to try: the limited-release Aurum Chardonnay and Chenin Avec Chêne; the Redhill Pinotage, Merindol Syrah and red blends, the flagship Tiara and the Frans Malan Cape Blend.

The lively tasting room is a friendly and inviting space, with a chandelier

"Over 40 years ago, my father, the late Frans Malan, left an indelible legacy by giving the country its first sparkling wine made according to the French tradition of secondary bottle fermentation."

Johan Malan, cellarmaster

made of wine glasses. Sit at the L-shaped yellowwood and imbuia counter or at the long stinkwood and yellowwood tables inside, where there is a crackling fire in the winter months. There are also wrought iron tables and chairs on the shady veranda, ideal for tasting on summer days, where old winemaking equipment, such as basket presses, is on display.

Simonsig's Cuvée restaurant (open all year for lunch Tuesday to Sunday; in summer for dinner Wednesday to Saturday; in winter for dinner Friday only), with its eclectic interior, and a terrace with mountain vistas, opened in 2008. Head chef Lucas Carstens honed his skills at Terroir in Stellenbosch and at Rueben's at the One & Only Hotel in Cape Town. He takes his inspiration from French Provençal, South African and fusion flavours for this seasonal menu with a sustainable conscience.

There's a kitchen garden and the carbon footprint is curtailed by relying mainly on local produce such as mushrooms from Jonkershoek and trout from Franschhoek. Each dish is paired with Simonsig's wines – the wine list showcases only wines from the estate but the offering is extensive, with rare vintages too.

SPIER

ADDRESS Baden Powell Drive (R310), Stellenbosch

GPS S 33° 58′ 24.63″ E 18° 47′ 2.23″

TEL +27 (0)21 809 1143

WEBSITE www.spier.co.za

TASTING & SALES Daily 10h00 – 16h30 (tasting) and 09h00 – 17h00 (sales)

AESTHETIC A rich heritage reinvigorated combines with contemporary South African culture, creating a multifaceted and dynamic tourism offering; a sustainable approach permeates the entire property

ATTRACTIONS Eight restaurant (farm-to-table ethos); Eight To Go & Picnics; Moyo at Spier; four-star Spier Hotel, Restaurant & Spa; Manor House Museum & The Heritage Walk; Gables Audio Walk; Protea Walk along the river bank; Segway two-wheeled gliding tours; Eagle Encounters; cellar tours

MUST DO Take a fascinating journey into Spier's past with a Gables Audio Walk or observe the national flower close-up on the beautiful Protea Walk; book a fun and informative Barrel Thief tasting

MUST TASTE Frans K. Smit flagship red blend, 21 Gables Chenin Blanc and Pinotage

The earliest owner of Spier, which dates back to 1692, was a German soldier in the service of the Dutch East India Company, Arnoud (or Aarnout) Jansz, who planted the first vines. Grapes were pressed on the farm for the first time in 1712. In 1971, then owner Neil Joubert began bottling wine under the Spier label – prior to this the wine made was sold to the larger co-operatives, such as Stellenbosch Farmers winery and the KWV. It was in this year too that he played a part in founding the Stellenbosch Wine Route.

While still strongly rooted in its heritage, today Spier offers a multifaceted wine tourism experience that reflects a vibrant culture. The warm African *wamkelekile* (welcome) is immediately evident in the welcoming smiles of the staff. A sustainable approach permeates every aspect of this farm, a WWF-SA Biodiversity & Wine Initiative Champion, where ongoing educational, business and ecological projects are conducted.

Spier has evolved into a destination that can keep you entertained for a full day or even an entire weekend. Every aspect of this historic property is brought to life for visitors.

If you have a penchant for gables you will be spoilt for choice at Spier which boasts no less than 21. Dr Hans Fransen, one of the Cape's leading architectural historians, wrote: "Of all Cape Dutch farms in the Cape, most of them with their own centre and end gables, it is Spier that boasts the greatest number of them: 21 in total, all beautifully preserved. As it happens, these 21 gables represent half a century of time and virtually the entire range of styles of that period. A leisurely walk around the farm will therefore amount to a lesson in art history."

Researched and written by playwright Brett Bailey, and narrated by Sannie de Goede, the 'ghost' of a slave who lived on Spier in 1836, the Gables Audio Walk is a fictionalised account of life on a Stellenbosch wine farm 200 years ago. Book and collect a headset and an audio device that takes you on an interactive history tour via 12 numbered stops along the pathways.

The highly informative Heritage Walk combines nature and history, as it wanders through the protea garden and the avenue of indigenous coral trees, and past buildings such as the 1822 manor house and South Africa's oldest dated wine cellar (1767). The Protea Walk meanders along the south bank of the Eerste River and gives you a chance to observe the large variety of proteas growing on the farm. Landscape architect Patrick Watson and horticulturist Wilton Sikhosana established this walk which celebrates our national flower.

On the far side of the estate you will find Eagle Encounters – a rehabilitation, conservation, education and eco-tourism project where you can have a personal encounter with these magnificent birds of prey and experience the unique interactive falconry flying shows.

And if you have a yen for adventure, a Segway Personal Transporter is a fun and eco-friendly way to see the farm, from the vineyards to the water treatment facility and the protea garden. An experienced guide first shows you the ropes and then accompanies you on the tour.

The vibrant Craft Market (open every day 10h00 – 17h00) showcases top-quality contemporary and traditional work by South African crafters, from beadwork and ceramics to pottery, textiles and wood-turned bowls. Spier Hotel with its village-style buildings also showcases artwork by local artists. The hotel is a pioneer in responsible tourism and was one of the first in the country to be awarded Fair Trade in Tourism SA accreditation in 2004.

Spier's Wine Welcome Centre, on the banks of the farm dam with a deck for al fresco tastings, features a chandelier by well-known Cape Town artist Heath Nash. Made from 334 recycled Spier wine bottles, it weighs in at a hefty 370 kg and hangs above the tasting counter. Inside seating options include chairs at long tables and comfy couches. Food and wine pairings offer a choice of charcuterie, cheese and olives.

The wines are tiered in several ranges, starting with the flagship red blend, Frans K. Smit, named after Spier's skilled cellarmaster. There's the 21 Gables range of Pinotage and Chenin Blanc, two varieties that Frans is passionate about, which references the unique gables on the farm. The Creative Block range was inspired by a Spier Arts Academy project that combines artworks from different artists and features three blends (2, 3 and 5) made from grapes selected from various vineyard blocks. Completing the line-up is the Méthode Cap Classique and the Signature range of popular everyday wines.

Spier follows biodynamic farm principles and has an extensive organic vegetable garden. Cattle, sheep and chicken are pasture-raised and eggs are free range. This natural produce is used in Spier's farm-to-table Eight restaurant (open for brunch and lunch Tuesday to Sunday) and Eight to Go deli (09h00 – 17h00).

Eight, which was designed according to Feng Shui principles, is a light-filled space with art on the walls and a ceiling, also designed by Heath Nash, covered in over 14 000 handcrafted flowers made from recycled white plastic milk bottles and embedded with energy-saving light bulbs. There's also a terrace outside, shaded by oak trees and perfect for sunny days. The country kitchen is headed by chef Lolli Heyns, whose à la carte lunch menu (May to November) features wholesome fare from salads to soups, chicken pies and roasts. In summer (December to April), the Harvest Table is laden with

delicious cold and hot dishes, as well as meat prepared on the braai outside. Plates are weighed to determine prices. Only Spier's wines feature on the winelist – these include organic wines to go with the fresh, healthy food.

Eight-to-Go next door offers ready-to-eat food, also prepared from local, natural and organic produce, from which you can select the makings of your own picnic. Or you can pre-book a picnic basket (24 hours in advance), created by Eight's chef Lolli in consultation with acclaimed foodie Judy Badenhorst; there's a range of choices from Gourmet to Relaxed, Vegetarian and Raw, as well as healthy children's picnics.

African-themed Moyo at Spier, an exotic venue with Bedouin-style tents and seating in the gardens or on treetop platforms, serves an extensive buffet featuring Pan-African dishes from tagines to potjies. At Spier Hotel, you can enjoy a meal at the well-appointed restaurant (open daily for breakfast and dinner) or a light meal or snacks with a glass of wine on the terrace at the wine bar.

STARK-CONDÉ WINES

"Crafting wine requires patience and the crazy belief that the shortest line between two points may not always be the right one." José Conde, cellarmaster

Businessman Hans Peter Schröder, who relocated to Stellenbosch after living in Japan for over two decades, bought Oude Nektar in the scenic Jonkershoek valley in the late 1980s. The name he gave the farm is a combination of his mother's maiden name (Stark) and that of his daughter Marie's husband, José Conde from Kansas City in the US, who handcrafts the wines at this small family-run winery.

Steep changes in vineyard elevation (from 150 to 600 metres above sea level) make for a range of sites with distinct characteristics. The valley with its high winter rainfall is ideally suited to Cabernet Sauvignon and other Bordeaux varieties. The Jonkershoek wines are often described as having lush fruit and fine, soft tannins.

José sticks to traditional winemaking methods, such as hand-picking, meticulous grape selection, basket pressing, open-tank fermentation, manual punch-downs and careful maturation in small French oak barrels, to produce the elegant wines Stark-Condé has become known for.

A wooden walkway leads to the tranquil tasting room, built in the style of a Japanese floating tea room. On its own small island in the middle of the dam, it has exceptional views of the surrounding vineyards and mountains. You can sit outside on the deck under the willow trees in good weather.

The Postcard Café (open for brunch and light lunches Tuesday to Sunday; closed on certain public holidays), run by Marie, is a lovely location for light meals – artisanal Oude Bank Bakkerij in Stellenbosch supplies the delicious bread. Or enjoy freshly baked cake and good coffee (supplied by Espresso Lab Microroasters in Woodstock; the Japanese-style iced coffee is perfect for a summer's day). It's best to book a table, preferably outside, and make sure you arrive on time as it's so popular they give tables away if customers are tardy. The restaurant serves the Stark-Condé wines at cellar-door prices (some are also available by the glass or carafe).

ADDRESS Jonkershoek Road, Stellenbosch

GPS S 33° 57' 14" E 18° 54' 38"

TEL +27 (0)21 887 3665

WEBSITE www.stark-conde.co.za

TASTING & SALES Daily 10h00 – 16h00 (closed Good Friday, 25 Dec & 1 Jan)

AESTHETIC Unique hand-built Japanese floating-style tasting room shaded by willow trees; picturesque valley views

ATTRACTIONS Postcard Café (Tues – Sun 09h30 – 16h00)

MUST DO Some of the wines are intriguing so take the time to savour them slowly in this tranquil fairy-tale setting

MUST TASTE The Three Pines Cabernet and Syrah stand out, but the handcrafted wines in all three small ranges are worth tasting

THELEMA MOUNTAIN VINEYARDS

"Thelema is, as far as we're concerned, one of the most beautiful places on earth, with great old oak trees, spectacular mountain views and colourful, noisy peacocks."
Gyles Webb, cellarmaster

This family owned and managed wine farm at the top of the Helshoogte Pass lives up to its name with vineyards clambering up the steep foothills of the Simonsberg mountain. Elevations ranging from 370 to 640 metres above sea level and predominantly south-facing slopes make it one of the coolest and highest farms in the area. This coupled with deep red soils make it ideal for growing top-quality grapes.

It was a taste of some Burgundy Puligny-Montrachet that persuaded former accountant Gyles Webb to move from Durban in KwaZulu-Natal to study winemaking at Stellenbosch University and, with the help of his wife Barbara's family, the McLeans, buy this once dilapidated fruit farm in 1983. Orchards made way for vineyards and the first wines under the Thelema label were released in 1988. Both the Webbs and the McLeans share the symbol of the phoenix in their family histories and this sacred mythological fire bird, which represents rebirth, became Thelema's crest.

By the mid-1990s, Thelema's wines were selling out within a month of release and some had achieved cult status. In 2000, Gyles took on the role of cellarmaster with Rudi Schultz stepping into the winemaking role. All the grapes vinified for the Thelema label are grown on the estate and the wines are bottled on the property too. Looking for a new challenge, in 2002 Gyles bought an apple farm in the cool-climate Elgin valley and converted it to vineyards. These grapes are also vinified at Thelema and destined for its Sutherland range. Thelema's wines have remained consistently excellent over the years.

In the modern tasting room, expect to feel right at home over a chat and a sampling of Thelema's wines, which include cult wine, The Mint Cabernet Sauvignon, with its distinct herbal profile. As the wines from each range contrast in character, it's interesting to compare, for example, a Thelema Sauvignon Blanc from Stellenbosch with a Sutherland Sauvignon Blanc from Elgin.

ADDRESS R310, Helshoogte Pass, Stellenbosch

GPS S 33° 54′ 30″ E 18° 55′ 23.4″

TEL +27 (0)21 885 1924

WEBSITE www.thelema.co.za

TASTING & SALES Mon – Fri 09h00 – 17h00; Sat 10h00 – 15h00

AESTHETIC An iconic South African wine farm; modern tasting room with views of mountainside vineyards; ever-present dogs welcome you to the farm

ATTRACTIONS BYO picnic

MUST DO It's all about the wines and the mountain views

MUST TASTE The cult Cabernet Sauvignons and the Merlot Reserve, which is one of the finest in the Cape

TOKARA

"All I wanted was a less hectic life in the country with a stream and some trout where I could go fishing. Instead, I ended up with a wine farm."

GT Ferreira, owner

From its vantage point at the crest of the Helshoogte Pass, Tokara has exceptional views, whichever way you look – there are vineyards and olive groves, valleys and mountains, from the Simonsberg to Table Mountain in the distance. The farm was purchased in 1994 by GT Ferreira, Chairman of RMB Holdings Limited, and his wife Anne-Marie. It was originally intended only for residential purposes but he soon saw the potential for winegrowing and classic varieties were planted on the slopes, which lie 400 metres above sea level. The farm takes its name from the couple's two children, Thomas and Kara.

Miles Mossop has been making wine in the glass-walled contemporary cellar since its inception in 2000, initially under the guidance of Gyles Webb of neighbouring Thelema (see page 152). Viticulturist Aidan Morton has also been at Tokara since the start. The first wines were bottled in 2001. Tokara has vineyards both at the Stellenbosch home farm and in cool-climate Elgin at Highlands farm and Walker Bay at Siberia in the Upper Hemel-en-Aarde valley. The Tokara wines are focused and site-specific, representing these three diverse and distinct prime winegrowing areas in the Reserve Collection and the Tokara range. Tokara also produces a small quantity of five-year-old potstill brandy, as well as extra virgin olive oils, which are available for tasting and purchase at Tokara Delicatessen.

The modern, award-winning architectural design of the winery and visitor facilities blends into the landscape and incorporates two wine tasting areas – the main one is busy and buzzy, more often than not filled with people from all corners of the globe, and the tasting counter can get quite crowded; the other is a private room (bookings only, for up to 12 people). At the entrance to the winery is a striking metal sculpture, The Mind's Vine by artist Marco Cianfanelli. All the spaces are filled with contemporary South African art representing both established and emerging talent, handcrafted furniture, stonework and various other design elements. On display in the tasting room is an immaculately restored Odobey turret clock, which was made in France (circa 1880).

ADDRESS Helshoogte Pass (R310), Stellenbosch

GPS S 33° 55' 5.13" E 18° 55' 15.29"

TASTING & SALES Mon – Fri 09h00 – 17h00; Sat/Sun 10h00 – 15h00 (closed on certain public holidays)

TEL +27 (0)21 808 5900

WEBSITE www.tokara.com

AESTHETIC Contemporary architecture; a busy tasting room with a huge stone fireplace and incredible views

ATTRACTIONS Tokara Restaurant; Delicatessen; art exhibitions

MUST DO Enjoy a glass of wine in a cosy armchair in front of a roaring fire in winter or on the balcony with its exceptional views in summer

MUST TASTE The Reserve Collection – it's interesting to compare the Chardonnays (one of Stellenbosch origin, the other Walker Bay) and the Sauvignon Blancs (Elgin and Walker Bay)

There's also a Sculpture Garden at the spacious and modern L-shaped Tokara Delicatessen (open for breakfast and lunch Tuesday to Sunday). Owned by Anne-Marie and daughter Kara, it is a relaxed, child-friendly eatery that offers simple, healthy meals made from organic, preservative-free farm produce. It's a great spot for breakfast or brunch. On weekends there's a lunch buffet, during the week there are quiches, sandwiches and burgers. A selection of Tokara wines is served, some by the glass. Children are well catered for with their own menus, a jungle gym and tree-house nests. Tokara's delicious olive oils and an array of deli items, from charcuterie, cheese and homemade pies to coffee, chocolates and gourmet fudge, among others, are available in the deli shop.

The sensational view from the Tokara Restaurant (open for lunch Monday to Sunday, dinner Tuesday to Saturday) is best enjoyed from the tables on the deck – you can see all the way to False Bay when the weather is good. Artworks add interest to the semi-industrial interior. Award-winning chef Richard Carstens impresses with his playful, well-presented dishes, many of which show Asian influences from his time spent working in the East. The menu is imaginative and consistently good. The excellent and extensive winelist was carefully compiled by sommelier Jaap-Henk Koelewijn.

VERGELEGEN WINES

ADDRESS Lourensford Road, Somerset West

GPS S 34° 4' 47" E 18° 53' 12.3"

TEL +27 (0)21 847 1334

WEBSITE www.vergelegen.co.za

TASTING & SALES Daily 09h00 – 18h00
(Oct – Apr); 09h00 – 17h00 (May – Sep)

AESTHETIC A national treasure with well-
preserved Cape Dutch buildings; exquisite
gardens, balm for the soul

ATTRACTIONS Camphors at Vergelegen;
Stables Restaurant, with an adventure
garden for children; Camphor Forest Picnic;
historic homestead and library; daily cellar
tours (Nov – Apr 10h15, 11h30 & 15h00;
May – Oct 11h30 & 15h00)

MUST DO Stroll through the extensive
gardens (18 in total), lingering along the
way to be captivated by 300-year-old
camphor trees; visit the historic
homestead with its exhibition corridor –
a knowledgeable custodian is available to
answer questions and provide fascinating
in-depth information

MUST TASTE The iconic flagship Vergelegen
Red and White (there's an additional
tasting fee but it's worth it)

Vergelegen has a long and illustrious history, stretching back to 1685 when it was most likely a military outpost. In early 1700, this freehold land was granted to Governor Willem Adriaan van der Stel, who transformed it into a flourishing estate with cattle stations, fruit orchards, orange groves and vineyards. The homestead, which has been immaculately restored and maintained, reflects the rich layered history of the Cape. It is fronted by five magnificent camphors planted by Van der Stel and these trees, thought to be over 300 years old, are the oldest living officially documented trees on the sub-continent. They were proclaimed National Monuments in 1942 and have an expected lifespan of another 150 to 200 years.

A succession of owners subsequently came and went until 1917, when Sir Lionel Phillips purchased the property for his wife Lady Florence Phillips, who set about transforming it. Vineyards were uprooted, gardens were planted, the historic homestead was renovated – it became a hub for high society and artists – and the old winery was converted into a library to house her husband's priceless collection of books. After their deaths, the Barlow family bought the property. They started a dairy herd, which became one of the largest and finest in the country, and planted extensive peach orchards.

Anglo American purchased the property in 1987. In the 26 years that it has owned the estate, the company has made extensive investment into planting vineyards – there are 158 hectares in total today – and also built a modern cellar. Anglo also restored the homestead, catalogued Sir Lionel's collection of rare books and in 1992 opened the estate's doors to share this national treasure with visitors from around the world. The homestead showcases early Cape furniture and other treasures, providing a glimpse into the three centuries of the farm's history. The library still houses Sir Lionel's collection of rare books, which includes Africana and French volumes. It's interesting to note that the lime-washed buildings are ochre-tinged, which is an authentic touch as river water was originally used to mix the paint.

The grounds were also developed and today there are 18 themed gardens for visitors to explore. These include the formal Octagonal Garden and Reflection Garden, Africa's first and only International Camellia Garden of Excellence (August is the time to view the pink, red and white blooms), the Rose Garden and Terrace, the Hydrangea Garden, Maple Tree Garden and Wetland Garden, and a fragrant Herb Garden. A more recent addition is the East Garden, which includes linear water features, a children's adventure playground, a maze constructed from ornamental vines, some 14 000 indigenous agapanthus plants massed in bands according to colour and

flowering times, and an oak arboretum. Vergelegen has a long history of oaks, from a hollow 300-year-old English oak, believed to be the oldest living oak in southern Africa, to the Royal Oak, planted in 1928 from one of the last acorns of King Alfred's oaks at Blenheim Palace. Acorns from it were in turn collected by his Majesty King George VI in 1947 for replanting at Windsor Great Park. There's a magical Camphor Forest, where you can picnic, and the Yellowwood Walk, with a yellowwood tree that was planted around 1700.

Vergelegen, a WWF-SA Biodiversity & Wine Initiative Champion, instituted an invasive alien vegetation clearing programme in 2004 to systematically restore 2 200 hectares of land to its natural flora and fauna. This is part of an ambitious ongoing multidimensional project, the largest privately funded conservation project in South Africa.

In contrast to the historical core of the estate, the octagonal gravity-flow cellar, built into a hill and blessed with exceptional 360-degree views from its rooftop, is totally modern. The first wine, following Anglo's comprehensive planting programme in the late 1980s, was produced at Vergelegen in 1992. Only two winemakers have held the position of cellarmaster: Martin Meinert, from 1988 to 1997, and the current incumbent, André van Rensburg.

The multi award-winning wine range, which includes the Flagship range of blends, a Reserve range and the Premium range, can be tasted in the thatch-roofed Tasting and Information Centre, which overlooks the Herb Garden. Its contemporary interior features a magnificent five-metre long yellowwood table.

The culinary team at Vergelegen aims to provide its visitors with world-class cuisine. Camphors at Vergelegen (lunch Wednesday to Sunday, dinner Friday and Saturday), with its elegant interior and an extended terrace overlooking the gardens, is the estate's signature 60-seater restaurant. The menu, which reflects classical local and international dishes, layered with flavour and given a modern treatment, offers choices of two or three courses, as well as a six-course tasting menu paired with wines. The gardens are planted to culinary herbs, vegetables, fruit and nuts, which the kitchen team puts to full use.

Bistro-style Stables (open for breakfast and lunch daily) has a contemporary country menu and its winelist features the full range of Vergelegen wines. Adjacent to the tasting centre and overlooking the East Garden, the restaurant is built on the site of what were once the old farm stables. Modern in design, with its thatched roof and timber beams it blends in with its Cape Dutch neighbours. The work of local artists adorns the walls. This laid-back eatery is perfect for family outings as it has a children's play area with a maze and beautiful wooden animals made locally of wood from the estate.

Vergelegen's Camphor Forest Picnics (November to April, bookings via Stables essential) offer a great selection of farm-crafted foods, to be enjoyed at tables in the shady forest.

*"Every season reveals
a new discovery ..."*
Richard Arm, horticulturist
and gardens manager

VILLIERA WINES

ADDRESS R304, Stellenbosch

GPS S 33° 50' 14.4" E 18° 47' 34.4"

TEL +27 (0)21 865 2002/3

WEBSITE www.villiera.com

TASTING & SALES Mon – Fri 09h00 – 17h00; Sat 09h00 – 15h00 (closed Good Friday & 25 Dec)

AESTHETIC An ethical approach permeates all aspects of this friendly family farm and wine business; the stylish Wine Sanctuary extends to a relaxed outdoor area for tasting under the trees

ATTRACTIONS Wildlife Sanctuary (book ahead for game drives and birding, which include wine tasting and cellar tour); Dalewood cheese platters or BYO picnic; self-guided cellar tours

MUST DO Book a guided game drive

MUST TASTE There's a wide selection of wine varieties and styles to choose from, from Méthode Cap Classique to white, red and blends (and often a wine or two from their French vineyards too), but the Monro Brut would make an excellent starting point

WINE TIP If you love bubbly but are prone to allergies or prefer yours free of additives, you can stock up on some Brut Natural

This family-owned and -run winery was started by cousins Jeff and Simon Grier in 1983. Jeff's sister, Cathy Grier Brewer, later joined them to head up the export, marketing and sales divisions. Today Villiera is one of the largest privately owned wineries in the country and a popular stop for locals and tourists alike.

Villiera is a member of the WWF-SA Biodiversity & Wine Initiative and the pioneering Grier clan is committed to preserving the environment. Villiera was the first winery to switch to solar power in 2010, and has one of the largest private roof-mounted photovoltaic installations in southern Africa. Viticulturist Simon, a keen environmentalist, employs ecologically friendly vineyard management practices, such as natural pest control via a huge flock of Peking ducks, water conservation, recycling and a greening project that entails the planting of thousands of indigenous trees on the farm, many of them *spekboom*, which are highly effective at sequestering carbon dioxide. There are 35 owl boxes in the vineyards too, populated by barn owls, crows and even swarms of bees. This eco-friendly philosophy has led to a healthy and vibrant eco-system on the farm, from flocks of guinea fowl and pheasant to steenbok, Cape and bat-eared foxes, water and grey mongooses, porcupine, caracals and the threatened blue crane.

A leisurely guided game drive (Monday to Saturday, pre-booked only) through the 220-hectare Villiera Wildlife Sanctuary takes around two hours and offers visitors a chance to experience game viewing just 40 minutes' drive from Cape Town's CBD. It was opened in 2009 in conjunction with two of Villiera's neighbours, Cape Garden Centre and Klawervlei. Once through its gates, marked by the skull of an antelope, visitors can get to see a variety of game. There are various antelope, Burchell's zebra, hartebeest and giraffe, as well as many smaller mammals and a huge diversity of birdlife, attracted to a dozen dams and marsh areas. More game is being introduced. A special sunset drive, complete with a wine tasting and supper, such as homemade venison pie with a tomato salad, is also a lovely option (in the summer months, by appointment only; check the website for dates, which are posted well in advance). A guide drives visitors in an electric-propelled vehicle that is recharged via the solar system and is used for vineyard work as well.

A total of 180 hectares of the 400-hectare property are planted to vineyards. Villiera specialises in Méthode Cap Classique (MCC), a fast-growing category. This was initiated in the mid-1980s via a 10-year partnership with Frenchman Jean-Louis Denois, a Champagne specialist. Today, Villiera's acclaimed range includes the Villiera Monro Brut and

the additive-free Villiera Brut Natural, the non-vintage Tradition Brut and Tradition Rosé Brut, and the first low-alcohol MCC, Starlight Brut. When it comes to white wines, there's a strong focus on Sauvignon Blanc and Chenin Blanc. Villiera has also built a reputation for Merlot and Cabernet Sauvignon, and there's a blend of the two, Monro, as well. The popular easy-drinking Down to Earth range comprises a white blend of Sauvignon and Semillon, and a Shiraz-based red blend. When conditions are favourable, Villiera produces a Noble Late Harvest dessert wine from Chenin Blanc and Riesling, called Inspiration, as well as a Late Bottled Vintage port-style wine, Fired Earth. All Villiera's wines offer great value.

The once rustic tasting room was renovated under the direction of architect Rick Stander and interior designer Liesel Rossouw. All materials from the old tasting room were recycled and low-consumption LED lighting was installed. Renamed The Wine Sanctuary, this stylish space features a chandelier by Willowlamp, a 'wine scene' lightbox by Leonora van Staden, and an 'ancient vine' metal panel crafted by Artvark in Kalk Bay. There is a terrace area in the shade of some old oak trees where you can enjoy an outdoor tasting. Try the unusual bubbly and nougat pairing experience, which partners Villiera MCCs with Sally Williams products (these are also available for purchase from the tasting room). One or two wines from their French vineyards, Domaine Grier, are often available for tasting too.

WARWICK ESTATE

"The saying goes that you can only make good wine if you can see Table Mountain from somewhere on your farm – which we can!"

Lawrence White, front-of-house manager

W arwick is family owned and family friendly – children are welcome at this relaxed farm where they can play on the grass and jungle gym, and even swim in the fountain on a hot day.

Warwick was known as De Goede Sukses from 1771 until 1902, when the Anglo-Boer war ended and it was bought by Colonel William Alexander Gordon, the commanding officer of the Warwickshire regiment, who renamed the farm Warwick as a tribute to his regiment.

Stan Ratcliffe purchased Warwick in 1964 and, together with his wife Norma, started planting Cabernet Sauvignon. The high-quality grapes were soon bought up by neighbouring wineries. Norma became more interested in winemaking and soon a cellar was in place where she began handcrafting her own wines using grapes from the farm. In 1984, she released her first wine, a Cabernet Sauvignon named La Femme Bleu (the Blue Lady). This was followed by a Bordeaux-style blend in 1986, the flagship Warwick Trilogy. Norma, one of the first women to make wine in South Africa and the first female member and only woman to date to chair the Cape Winemakers Guild, is still involved in all aspects of the family wine business. Son Mike Ratcliffe is the general manager.

Warwick is the only estate open 365 days a year. Tastings are personal and conducted by wine advisors, who are unhurried and informative and will take you through the range and tell you the stories behind the wines.

Varietal wines include an oaked Chardonnay, Professor Black Sauvignon Blanc, The First Lady Unoaked Chardonnay, the First Lady Cabernet Sauvignon (Norma is often referred to as the First Lady for her pivotal role in the development of the wine industry in South Africa), a Cabernet Franc, the Old Bush Vines Pinotage and the Black Lady Syrah. A Bordeaux-style blend, Trilogy, and the notorious Three Cape Ladies, a Cape blend sipped by James Bond in the latest novel, *Carte Blanche*, complete the ranges. Warwick is one of the few wineries where old and rare vintages are still available for sampling. You can also taste wine out of The Wedding Cup (designed by the estate, these are available for purchase too) and hear the romantic tale of the King

ADDRESS R44, Stellenbosch

GPS S 33° 50' 27" E 18° 51' 54"

TEL +27 (0)21 884 4410

WEBSITE www.warwickwine.com

TASTING & SALES Daily 10h00 – 17h00

AESTHETIC A relaxed and welcoming destination with a reputation for the best gourmet picnics in the winelands

ATTRACTIONS 'Big 5' Vineyard Safari; gourmet picnics in summer and tapas menu in winter; cellar tours (by appointment)

MUST DO Take a fun 'Big 5' Vineyard Safari in a game vehicle or on horseback; picnic in the privacy of one of the custom-designed 'pods' (booking required for both options)

MUST TASTE Professor Black Sauvignon Blanc, the single-varietal bottling of Cabernet Franc, a benchmark, and the flagship Bordeaux-style blend, Trilogy

and Queen of Nuremberg's daughter, the beautiful Princess Kunigunde, who was betrothed to a prince from a faraway kingdom but fell in love with a handsome young silversmith.

There's plenty to see and do at this innovative boutique winery. You can book an entertaining and educational 'Big 5' Vineyard Safari – a guide takes you through the vineyards in a 4x4 game vehicle but instead of spotting the traditional 'Big 5' you identify Warwick's 'big five' varieties: Cabernet Sauvignon, Cabernet Franc, Merlot, Pinotage and Sauvignon Blanc. Each one is then compared to one of the 'Big 5' – the Cabernet Sauvignon, for example, is likened to a lion. The guide stops at each vineyard, explaining the different varieties and terroir, giving visitors real insight into the winegrowing process. You get to taste the wine too on this mountain journey with its unrivalled winelands views all the way to Table Mountain. The 'Big 5' safari is also available on horseback for the more adventurous.

Warwick's gourmet picnics have a well-deserved reputation as the best in the winelands. It's hard to beat lounging around on over-sized cushions on the lawn at the dam while being served by a picnic butler. There's also the Forest Courtyard, adjacent to the fountain and jungle gym for those wishing to keep an eye on their children. If you want more privacy, you can book one of the funky designer pods, which seat up to 12 picnickers. The prettily presented gourmet picnics come enclosed in an eco-friendly cardboard box tied with a ribbon.

WATERFORD ESTATE

ADDRESS Blaauwklippen Road,
Stellenbosch

GPS S 33° 59' 52.54" E 18° 87' 06.15"

TEL +27 (0)21 880 5300

WEBSITE www.waterfordestate.co.za

TASTING & SALES Mon – Fri 09h00 – 17h00;
Sat 10h00 – 17h00 (closed on certain
public holidays)

AESTHETIC A sensory experience; honeyed
stone walls, clementine groves and
lavender beds evoke the south of France

ATTRACTIONS The Waterford Wine Drive
& Porcupine Trail Walk (both two hours'
duration, pre-booking essential); boules in
the courtyards; cellar tours

MUST DO Try the decadent Wine and
Chocolate Experience, which Waterford is
famous for; relax in the comfy depths of a
couch in the courtyard or at the fireside –
it's all about a leisurely pace and lingering
over a glass of wine

MUST TASTE Waterford's flagship, The Jem
(there's an additional fee for tasting this)
or try the Reserve Vintage Tasting, which
culminates in a tasting of this complex
wine, a velvety red blend of 11 varieties

Turn into the driveway at Waterford Estate and a sensory journey begins. Ducks paddle across a pond, and groves of clementines and fragrant lavender beds lead up to the red-tiled winery. Situated near the top of the picturesque Blaauwklippen valley, the winery is built around a courtyard with Waterford Estate's trademark fountain at the centre. In summer, there are cushions so that you can sit on the low stone walls that surround it, watching games of boules in progress, and wide shady verandas for tasting in comfort. On chilly Cape winter days you can settle into comfy deep couches and armchairs in front of a roaring fire to enjoy tasting indoors. The winery, designed by Alex Walker, was created from quarried local bedrock, stones from the vineyards and timber grown on the estate. The cellar tour takes you through the winemaking process and into the lovely ambience of the barrel maturation cellar, dimly lit by chandeliers.

Founded in 1998, Waterford Estate is a partnership between two families who share the same dream and philosophy of embracing family, friends, food and wine. Jeremy and Leigh Ord (who put the 'ord' into Waterford) purchased the property, which was a part of the Stellenrust farm, and Kevin and Heather Arnold developed Waterford into the world-class wine estate it is today.

The small cellar team is headed by cellarmaster Kevin, who has a wealth of experience, having started out as winemaker at Delheim, where he spent nine years, and 10 years at Rust en Vrede. The estate produces 75 per cent red and 25 per cent white wines. There's the Waterford Estate range, with its flagship The Jem, which was released in 2007. None was made in 2008; the next release was in 2009. The Library Collection comprises a white and three red blends, the Waterford Estate range includes the much-lauded Kevin Arnold Shiraz, and the everyday Pecan Stream range comprises two whites and a red blend.

Waterford Estate offers an exceptional cellar-door experience, for which it has garnered both local and international awards. Visitors, who are encouraged to spend time both in the vineyards and the winery, get to really experience life on a working wine farm.

The Standard Tasting includes wines from the Waterford Estate range, the Kevin Arnold Shiraz and Pecan Stream range. The Wine and Chocolate Experience, presented by a tasting room attendant, pairs Waterford Estate wines with chocolates specially crafted by master chocolatier Richard von Geusau. A deliciously spicy example is the Kevin Arnold Shiraz with Masala Chai Dark Chocolate. The Waterford Estate Cabernet Sauvignon is paired with Rock Salt Dark Chocolate and the dessert wine, Waterford Estate Heatherleigh (named after Jeremy and Kevin's wives) is paired with Rose

Geranium Milk Chocolate. The Vintage Reserve Tasting (pre-booked only) is an informative, in-depth tutored tasting that includes some experimental wines, giving tasters an insight into the evolution of Waterford Estate's wines, leading up to the tasting of The Jem.

The Waterford Estate Wine Drive (pre-booking essential) is a more adventurous outdoors option. A two-hour trip in a 10-seater safari-style game-viewing Land Rover takes you through the estate and up onto the slopes of the Helderberg, where you can taste the estate's wines overlooking the vineyards of their origin. A guide takes you through all aspects of biodiversity and viticulture. The drive takes you past Pecan Stream, which is one of Waterford Estate's labels, and past Pebble Hill, the name of a red blend that falls under the same label. Wines are accompanied by snacks such as crusty fresh-baked bread with good olive oil, the plumpest of green olives, cashew nuts, and biltong and *droëwors*. Tasting outdoors with views of vineyards and mountains, from the Helderberg all the way to Table Mountain, is as good as it gets. For the more active, the Waterford Estate Porcupine Walking Trail is a two-hour guided walk that leaves from the cellar door and takes guests through fynbos and vineyards to the wild olive grove valley. A backpack with your selected wine and a light snack is provided.

WATERKLOOF

ADDRESS Sir Lowry's Pass Village Road, Somerset West

GPS S 34° 5' 55.4" E 18° 53' 22.8"

TEL +27 (0)21 858 1292

WEBSITE www.waterkloofwines.co.za

TASTING & SALES Daily 10h00 – 17h00

AESTHETIC A 'cellar in the sky' surrounded by a natural amphitheatre of mountains and vineyards, with views that are as striking as the clean-lined architecture; biodynamic, sustainable and conservation-minded

ATTRACTIONS The Restaurant at Waterkloof; art collection on display; walking/hiking trails; tutored horse-riding trails followed by a wine tasting and Ploughman's platter at the Tasting Lounge

MUST DO Take a walk and observe the Percheron horses at work; admire the views over False Bay to Cape Point

MUST TASTE Circle of Life Red and White; Circumstance Syrah

The driveway leading up to Waterkloof on the foothills of the Schapenberg is now tarred all the way and passes free-ranging 'veldlander' chickens, giving you a first inkling of what's to come at this farm, which is run on biodynamic principles.

Completed in 2009, Waterkloof's striking and modern concrete-and-glass winery cantilevers out from its hilltop site, maximising the dramatic views of vineyards, mountains and all the way over False Bay to Cape Point. It's often referred to as the 'cellar in the sky' and when you're sitting in the glass-box fine dining area you can watch raptors circling or catching the updrafts.

A bold metal tree sculpture by world-renowned land artist Strijdom van der Merwe stands five metres tall at the entrance to the cellar. The Blowing Man, which represents Boreas, the god of the north wind, also made of corroded steel, features both on the cellar wall and as Waterkloof's symbol (although it's the south-easter that blows in from False Bay just four kilometres away and cools these vineyards). Inside, the visitor facilities feature large-scale artworks by South African artists such as Richard Smith, Helmut Starcke, Pamela Stretton and Shany van den Berg.

Owner Paul Boutinot, who refers to himself as the custodian of Waterkloof, is an English wine merchant of French descent. In 1980 he founded Boutinot, the highly successful UK-based producer, importer and distributor. A management buy-out in March 2012 saw him step down to focus on Waterkloof, a private investment he made in 2003 after actively searching for the right vineyard site to make his desired fine wines that are in natural balance.

These steep hillside slopes in a natural mountain amphitheatre are farmed following sustainable biodynamic principles. Farm manager and viticulturist Christiaan Loots is committed to biodynamic farming methods and all the vineyards have now been converted. The biodiversity on the farm, which achieved WWF-SA Biodiversity & Wine Initiative Champion status in 2008, has been increased through the setting up of fynbos corridors that link the natural vegetation. The tractors have been replaced with a growing stable of Percherons, which are working draught horses. Horse-drawn spray pumps further reduce the use of heavy machinery in the vineyards. Ladybirds and wasps control pests such as mealybugs. Free-ranging chickens also help control vine pests, while simultaneously putting nitrogen back into the soil. Manure from their flock of sheep and four cows provides compost.

The ultra-modern gravitational cellar, which makes full functional use of the steep incline, has glass walls that reveal wooden open-top fermenters

and large barriques. Winemaker Nadia Barnard is a traditionalist who follows a minimal intervention approach and uses only the natural yeasts of the vineyards for fermentations. Elegance, restraint, integrity and food friendliness are the hallmarks of these wines.

The wines are ranged in three collections. The Waterkloof collection currently comprises only a Sauvignon Blanc, which is made in limited quantities from two windswept blocks at the top of the Schapenberg. It is only released in exceptional vintages and not always available. This singular Sauvignon is capable of ageing well over a number of years. Circle of Life showcases nature's ongoing cycle at this biodynamic farm and encompasses the flagship red and white blends. Circumstance is a range of single varietal wines, currently eight in total. Also made at Waterkloof is the False Bay Vineyards brand of everyday wines from selected vineyards across the winelands of the Western Cape, which includes the False Bay Vineyards and Peacock Ridge ranges.

Waterkloof's tasting lounge with its glass walls affords visitors views of both the working cellar and farm below. The lounge has a huge circular steel fireplace, which was designed by Frank Böhm. Surrounded by stylish leather furniture to lounge on, it is a focal point and a source of warmth for winter. On warm, wind-free days you can sit on the glassed-in balcony. Along with the wine tasting you can sample the slow-aged nine-, 12- or 18-months matured Healey's Cheddar, which is available for purchase here too, paired with a selection of Waterkloof wines. There's also a Ploughman's Platter on offer in the tasting lounge (10h00 to 15h00).

The Restaurant at Waterkloof (lunch and dinner Monday to Saturday, lunch only on Sunday) extends from the tasting lounge into a glass promontory that seats 120 guests. French chef Gregory Czarnecki who hails from Burgundy heads up the open-plan kitchen. Classical cuisine with a modern edge is exquisitely presented. In line with the ethos of the farm, only the freshest of ingredients are used, from free-range eggs and farm-reared lamb to veggies and herbs sourced from the kitchen garden on the farm. The provenance of ingredients sourced from further afield, such as Saldanha mussels or Magaliesberg duck breast, is apparent on the menu too. There's an á la carte and a dégustation menu, which change daily and feature a wine recommendation for each dish. Only wines from Waterkloof are listed but with several ranges and an abundance of perfect food partners there are plenty of options. Complimentary spring water from Waterkloof is also on offer.

Wellington

The warm-hearted town of Wellington, named after the Duke of Wellington who defeated Napoleon at Waterloo, is at the centre of this burgeoning wine district, which is a 45-minute drive from Cape Town. Surrounded by towering mountains and flanked by rivers, the valley has excellent soils and a favourable climate for winegrowing. Its vine-cutting nurseries supply 95 per cent of the wine industry, which means that most South African wines are effectively 'born' here.

The first farms were granted to Dutch free burghers in 1687 and a year later to French Huguenots. Known as Val du Charron or the

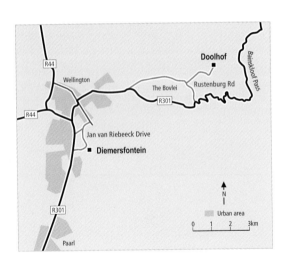

Valley of the Wagonmakers, it was once the last outpost before the wagons ventured on the long and often hazardous journey towards the interior.

There's a diversity of flora and fauna to be seen on wine walks through the fynbos, vineyards, orchards and olive groves of this friendly valley, as well as game drives and single-track mountain biking trails. Handmade cheeses and organic olive products are also available for tasting and purchase.

All the wineries are in easy driving distance of one another on this compact wine route. If you're a rugby fanatic, pay a visit to Welbedacht Wine Estate, home of Schalk Burger & Sons. Schalk Snr and Schalk Jnr are the eighth father-and-son in South Africa to be capped as Springboks, and paraphernalia highlighting their rugby careers is displayed in the tasting room.

There's also a restaurant, No. 6, on the property. Several wineries are by appointment only – it is certainly worth the effort to book a tasting at Bosman Family Vineyards with its historic *werf* if you are going to be in the area. Also by appointment only and worth a visit is Jorgensen's Distillery, where an artisanal range of premium spirits is crafted by Roger Jorgensen at the family farm, Versailles, in Wellington.

Also of interest

BOSMAN FAMILY VINEYARDS **www.bosmanwines.com**
JORGENSEN'S DISTILLERY **www.jd7.co.za**
NABYGELEGEN PRIVATE CELLAR **www.nabygelegen.co.za**
WELBEDACHT WINE ESTATE **www.schalkburgerandsons.co.za**
WELLINGTON WINE ROUTE **www.wellington.co.za**
WELLINGTON WINE WALK **www.winewalk.co.za**

Diemersfontein Wines

Located on the outskirts of Wellington, this third-generation family estate encompasses a wine farm, residential estate, guesthouse accommodation in the original Diemersfontein homestead with its large shady *stoep* and magnificent gardens, as well as a spa.

The Sonnenberg family has owned Diemersfontein since 1943, when current owner David's grandfather, Max, bought the 183-hectare farm with its panoramic views as a country retreat.

Max, together with his son Richard (David's father), was the co-founder of Woolworths South Africa and a Member of Parliament in the Jan Smuts era. During the war years Italian prisoners of war were billeted on the farm and the family's long association with the arts started with the strains of opera singing drifting up from their cottages. The family tradition of being patrons and contributors to the arts has been upheld by David and his wife Susan.

Richard took over the farm in the 1950s and became more involved in the farming operations. He planted the first vineyards in the 1970s. David built his own cellar in 2000 and started producing estate wines.

The tasting room has views over the dam and paddocks onto the granite-domed Paarl Mountain. Diemersfontein's trademark is Pinotage and a highlight on the social calendar is the annual Pinotage on Tap festival. The trend-setting 'coffee and chocolate' Pinotage was created here just over a decade ago, opening a new wine category with an ever-growing consumer fan base (and its fair share of detractors too). The wine's coffee aroma profile is achieved through a combination of oak, toasting and yeast. Seasons, the adjacent restaurant (open for lunch and dinner Tuesday to Sunday), lives up to its name by offering dishes using fresh, local and seasonal produce.

Also available for tasting is the Thokozani range of wines. *Thokozani* means 'celebration' and that's exactly the spirit in which this empowerment project was launched in 2005. Thokozani has several facets: there's the wine produced on the estate; conferencing; and guest cottages.

As a member of WWF-SA Biodiversity & Wine Initiative, Diemersfontein is committed to minimising further loss of its endangered renosterveld and striving towards using better, more sustainable farming and wine production methods. It's an ideal location for the rescued angulate tortoises (either saved from veld fires or surrendered to the Cape of Good Hope SPCA Wildlife Unit). Each one has been numbered to monitor its movements as far as possible. Diemersfontein is home to various other animals rescued by the unit too – Cape grysbok, kestrels and owls are often encountered on the farm.

*"Our coffee and
chocolate Pinotage is like
Marmite; either you love
it or you hate it."*
David Sonnenberg, owner

Doolhof Wine Estate

ADDRESS Rustenburg Road, The Bovlei, Wellington

GPS S 33° 37' 34.9" E 19° 4' 58.6"

TEL +27 (0)21 873 6911

WEBSITE www.doolhof.com

TASTING & SALES Mon–Sat 10h00–17h00; Sun 10h00–16h00 (closed on certain public holidays)

AESTHETIC Elegantly restored manicured property situated in the beautiful Bovlei valley below scenic Bainskloof Pass

ATTRACTIONS Five-star Grande Dédale Country House; cellar door menu; pre-booked picnic baskets; river walking trail and hikes; part of Wellington Wine Walk (private groups); mountain biking; cellar tours (by appointment)

MUST DO Walk the labyrinth and the river trail

MUST TASTE The Minotaur, the flagship Cape blend in the Legends of the Labyrinth range

It is a bit of a drive, including a section of dirt road, up to Doolhof, which is at the very top of the scenic Bovlei 'upper valley'. On the way are a couple of boutique wineries worth a look in, starting with Nabygelegen Private Cellar, where the old cellar dates back to the early 1800s and has been restored to make use of the ancient vats and underground tanks.

The valley is filled with history. The settlers who first laid eyes on the farm's many hills and vales in the early Eighteenth century named it Doolhof, an Afrikaans word meaning labyrinth. This landscape was utilised to make the best of the many varying micro-climates when positioning the vineyards.

In 1707 the first settlers grazed cattle here. Permits were granted from 1709 and formal freehold was granted in 1712 to Jacques Portier from Flanders, making him the first official owner of the property designated as Doolhof. Grapes for wine and brandy making were introduced by Huguenot settlers as early as 1728. After Portier's death in 1739, the farm passed through the hands of various owners including the well-known Retief family.

Andrew Geddes Bain built the famous Bainskloof Pass in the 1840s as, due to being surrounded on three sides by mountains, Wellington had no main route into the hinterland of South Africa. He lived on Doolhof, which traverses the pass, for part of the project. The pass was declared a National Monument in 1980.

Doolhof's wine legacy was revived in 1995 when the first contemporary vineyards were planted. In 2003, British couple Dennis and Dorothy Kerrison purchased the property and set about building a winery and tasting venue. In 2005, the cellar was completed, the farm was registered as an estate and the first wines under the Doolhof label were launched. There are now three ranges: Signatures of Doolhof, Legends of the Labyrinth and the Cape range.

Grand Dédale Country House, Wellington's first five-star guest lodge, is housed in the restored original manor house and opened its doors in 2009. The elegant tasting room was renovated recently too. Light lunches are available here from Tuesday to Sunday (pre-book for groups of six and more).

The River Walk meanders along the Kromme River for several kilometres and visitors can stop at any of the designated picnic sites along the way to enjoy the scenic views. There's also a 10-kilometre walk through the vineyards. Doolhof is home to many small animals, including buck and porcupines, which you may just spot along the way.

INDEX